# The Deacon Wore Spats

# The Deacon

*Profiles from America's*

# Wore Spats

## Changing Religious Scene

## John T. Stewart

Holt, Rinehart and Winston

New York   Chicago

San Francisco

Designer: Ernst Reichl
88150–0115
Printed in the United States of America

FOR INEZ

# Contents

# Introduction

This book represents one man's recollections of two-thirds of a century of American Protestantism. It is not a church history in any formal or complete sense, but the memoir of a participant— a church member from boyhood, later an ordained minister. As a man who has been pastor of several churches, chiefly Methodist and Congregational, I cannot muster the cool detachment of the spectator. But as a newspaperman, I had to tell it the way it was, without fear or favor, and most of this book could not have been written except by the reporter in me. It is all factual. I was there. The information comes partly from the memories of a lifetime, but much of it is tangible, from files that go back decades: annotated church calendars; news clippings of stories I wrote for the old *St. Louis Star,* the *St. Louis Post-Dispatch,* more recently *United Church Herald;* personal correspondence; and other memorabilia.

When the century opened, American Protestants looked out upon their world and saw that it was good. For them, it was indeed good. The deacon in his cutaway and spats was our best-dressed citizen, esteemed by all; and his ministerial counterpart was a genteel ambassador of the gospel of *noblesse oblige.* I have seen those images transformed during the past half century—and the change was not for the worse.

As a religious news editor, it was my job to write and edit the ups and downs of church news, to interview great men of the pulpit, to be present at many of the churches' historic conventions, and also to serve as the newspaper's "sermon shopper," keeping in touch with what ministers were preaching in cities and towns on Sundays. I have heard politicians preach sermons, and I have heard ministers preach politics and much else—including the gospel. By and large, they played it by ear in the best American tradition. If God had a pattern for the time, it was not visible at close range, and in this book I have not sought to impose one of my own.

I am glad to have been a witness to these events. In the early years, religious news seldom hit the front page; I have seen it grow in importance through times of both boom and decline. It has not been a lonely task, and I must pay tribute to men of many creeds and races with whom I shared it—fellow newsmen and fellow ministers, mostly the latter. It was not merely a spiritual sharing. We sat together at solemn assemblies, sneaking out for coffee and informal talk far from the bishop's august ear. We shared hotel rooms and Pullman berths and plane seats. We swapped stories and books, razor blades, food and clothing. Nobody has better friends than I have found among America's ministers. When they were poor—which was most of the time—they were very rich. It was a great life.

JOHN T. STEWART

# PART ONE

# 1

## Brush Arbors
## and Circuit Riders

In the years at the turn of the century when my brother Paul and I walked the mile and a quarter to Sunday school, we often stopped to look in imaginative wonder at the hump of soil in the field beside the lane where an early white settler and an Indian were buried together after they had shot each other down in a sudden encounter. The Indian had stalked the white man from inside a shock of cornstalks. But the wary white man was suspicious of a corn shock standing where he had never seen one before. When he raised his rifle to fire, the Indian leaped from his hiding and fired too. It was the beautiful wisdom of the little pioneer Methodist community that buried the white man and the Indian side by side where they fell—maybe their hates and fears would be buried too, and peace would come to stay. It did just that.

The twin graves lay on the wooded section of land which had been claimed and settled in 1812 by Alexander McCreery, a distant kinsman of mine, born in Kentucky in 1793 during the administration of President George Washington. He lived until 1884, nine years before I was born. Alexander and I both heard one Methodist circuit rider whose story I have to tell, Brother Davis.

The McCreerys came from Scotland to Virginia, then crossed

3

the Cumberland Gap into Kentucky. When Kentucky became
too crowded for Daniel Boone and his homestead-hunting neighbors, Boone pushed on into Missouri, and the McCreerys to
southern Illinois. There was little religion and no piety at all in
the band of settlers that cleared the Middle West of Indians,
timber, and topsoil. The pioneer preachers who followed them
had a hard time of it, trying to interest land-hungry families in
laying up treasure in heaven. Those men and women settlers
wanted first to know where their next meal was coming from.
Most of the preachers died early of exposure, loneliness, a poor
diet, or malarial fever.

Alexander McCreery was the indomitable leader of one of
those bands. He had gone back to Kentucky in 1817 to marry
Ann Harrell and brought his bride to southern Illinois on horse-
back—I played many hours on the long porch of the log house
where they lived together sixty-seven years. Their most precious
possessions—beyond their stout hearts—were his long-barreled
rifle and axe and her iron skillet. When the first Methodist
preacher reached their neighborhood, riding his horse and carrying saddlebags, the first man he looked up was Alexander: the
purpose, to start a church. The pioneer farmer stared at the
stranger and said, "You'd better throw away that Bible and get
an axe."

But the saddlebags preacher was persistent, and so was Aunt
Ann. In 1823 Alexander became a charter member of my
grandparents' church, Zion Methodist Episcopal Church in the
Roberts Settlement six miles south, in what became Williamson
County. Three years later, Alexander was the leading spirit in
the organization of a church on his own land, a quarter-mile
north of his house—Liberty Methodist Episcopal Church, where
my story begins.

For fifty-eight years Alexander sat in the amen corner—three
long pews at front left and at right angle to the other pews, at
the end of the pulpit and facing the reed organ and choir opposite. I grew up thinking there was more dignity and authority in
the amen corner than in the Supreme Court of the United States.

Those eight or ten old men didn't sit in awe of their preacher; he stood and preached in awe of them. When he rose to begin his sermon he could see out of the corner of his eye the Bibles lying open on their laps. Nearly every year some elder disappeared from the amen corner to lie in the churchyard, and the next Sunday his place was taken by the next man whom the congregation chose to honor. Today, a hundred and thirty-nine years later, Liberty Church carries on without interruption, its white frame sanctuary and the expanding cemetery beginning under the north windows maintained in perfect condition.

Sixty-five years ago the preaching and practice of religion were not under the austere eye and ear of amen corners any more than now. I can recall brush arbor meetings under forest trees and torchlight, with wood chips in place of sawdust in the aisles, and the revivals ("protracted meetings" they were called), which were held every summer after the corn was laid by. The Liberty congregation boycotted brush arbor meetings; the long services were too noisy and the crowds were irreverent—and "common," a word that fell with devastating effect when I heard it spoken to describe a scalawag neighbor. When the Free Will Baptists started a church across the road from our district school, the Methodists called them "common." Our minister was an educated man; theirs was a squatter on a hard-scrabble farm and sold lightning rods for a living.

Attending a brush arbor revival meant sitting on a bare plank without a back rest, fighting mosquitoes, and standing up every few minutes to let somebody in or out of the row. The congregation was constantly changing throughout the two or three hours—women took their crying babies out, men took themselves out. Men brought their buggy whips into the meeting and held them like a beggar's staff—if the tasseled whips were left in the dashboard sockets, they wouldn't be there when the meeting was over. Sometimes harnesses were slashed with a knife or a horse's tail left tied in a painful knot. Fist fights were frequent in the darkness under the trees; if brass knuckles were used, the fight was short and bloody.

The last brush arbor meeting I attended was in the 1920s, several years after I had left the farm and Liberty Church. I went with a cousin and her husband. We were late; there was a big crowd inside the enclosure and a bigger one outside. While our driver was cruising about trying to find a safe parking place, his car lights fell upon a young couple locked in a most compromising embrace on the back seat of a car. Our driver remarked, "Sometimes I think more souls are born than reborn from these brush arbor meetings." A few years later, at Harvard Divinity School, I heard George Foot Moore, our most distinguished professor, pass the same remark to his class of young men. Moore was a country boy too, from the Pennsylvania hills.

The earliest preaching I heard was by Methodist circuit riders at the turn of the century. They served the little white frame churches that dotted the countryside, three or four congregations yoked in a single pastorate known as a "charge." The minister usually moved on after a year or two, his stock of earthly goods hauled in a borrowed wagon, and he and his family riding in his buggy or surrey. A sermon every two weeks or once a month and the annual two-week revival were about all the pastoral care provided. But it was better preaching in 1901 than the same congregations were to hear for fifty years. Rural churches were already in calamitous decline under the circuit-riding system. Fierce rivalry among the denominations kept all churches and their budgets small, and as a result a professionally trained ministry virtually disappeared from the rural scene for more than a generation. Ironically, it was the old, established churches, the white Anglo-Saxon Protestants, who suffered most; immigrant churches—Roman Catholic, Lutheran, German Evangelical and German Reformed—built only where they already had communities or parishes.

Many of those early circuit riders were men of college and seminary training who read the New Testament in Greek; a few could even read Old Testament Hebrew. Some circuit riders wrote books, and all of them had modest libraries, just as nine out of ten of their church families didn't. They were paid six hundred dollars a year, some of it in kind.

There was little doctrinal preaching—Methodists didn't go heavily for doctrine; they were evangelists and reformers and pragmatists and ever hopeful. We got many sermons on patriotism and thrift and honesty and truth-telling and neighborliness and child discipline and Sabbath observance and church loyalty. The vanishing breed of dignified circuit riders wrote their sermons in longhand, though they nearly always preached from notes. They followed the nineteenth-century educated man's discipline of writing, which has been abandoned by most of the Th.D. clergy. Writing their sermons was, however, no great hardship for the older generation. An average pulpit career of forty years meant at least twenty different churches, so all that was needed was two years' supply in the old sermon barrel.

Sixty years ago the churches and clergy—like politics, medicine, newspapering, and the barlow-scarred bench in front of the general store—were enlivened by "characters" the likes of whom churchgoers of the 1960s never see or hear. Nonconformists were as thick as fiddlers in hell. The one I most vividly and fondly remember was Brother Davis.

He was a tall, spare, handsome military figure of a man who wore a full beard from the day he left the theological seminary. He was the only minister in a hundred years to serve my family church twice—the first time when he was graduated from the seminary and came to his first circuit charge, the second a return engagement more than thirty years later. In between, this gentleman and genuine scholar had made no material progress in his sacred calling. Brother Davis's sermons were not evangelistic enough to please his ecclesiastical superiors, who were more interested in numbers. He was respected and honored but unrewarded. He could quote the Bible and Shakespeare and Milton by the yard but was indifferent to rank and status; he had a quick wit and sharp tongue. And behind his proud back he was called a dude.

In his perdurable prime Brother Davis drove a fast-stepping span of matched bay horses and a high-wheeled buggy, and wore a linen duster over his claw-hammer coat, and yellow gloves. During his first pastorate at our country church he wore a top hat, but when he returned years later he had exchanged it for a stylish black fedora.

Like most dignified preachers of his day, Brother Davis carried an enormous white handkerchief in a hidden pocket in the long tail of his coat. From time to time while preaching he would thrust his hand deep in the folds of his coattail and jerk out his handkerchief with such a violent motion that it snapped full-length at his side like a small sail in the wind. (Little boys from the congregation practiced this wonderful trick for hours at home.) Then he brought his handkerchief to his nose with a sweeping gesture, blew his nose with the blast of a foghorn, and returned his handkerchief casually to the skirts of his long coat.

The most famous sermon Brother Davis ever preached was a monologue—a dramatic portrayal of little David slaying the giant Goliath. He presented his half-hour act in scores of churches over a period of forty years; it is still remembered by elderly members of the congregations he served. In recent years I have heard dramatic pulpit monologues by some half-dozen preachers; only once did the unconventional performance come off. Present-day churchgoers are too much accustomed to movies and television to be impressed by an amateur actor, even one with the holiest intentions.

Brother Davis took the entire twenty-foot pulpit platform in our little country church for his David-and-Goliath act. He impersonated the strutting, boastful Philistine giant and the shy but brave little shepherd lad. When the preacher's Goliath taunted the army of Israel his voice roared like a lion; David's voice was a boy's treble—like the shepherd's pipe. When, at the end, Goliath fell face downward with a stone from David's sling buried in his forehead, Brother Davis flung himself upon the pulpit's rag carpet with tremendous abandon and clatter. Then he leaped to his feet and, impersonating David, leaped upon his prostrate foe, drew Goliath's sword from its sheath and, as Scripture says, "cut off his head therewith."

Although I saw Brother Davis's dramatic monologue two or three times, I have forgotten what the moral of the sermon was supposed to be. But it was good fun for a little boy who was bored to his aching back by adult-sized oak pews and giant-sized sermons.

Not all preaching in the early years of this century was Emersonian in content and manner or shivering to the spine from dramatic delivery. Far from it. The ministry included both regularly ordained men who had passed educational and character tests, and volunteers and part-time parsons. (The Methodists and Presbyterians enforced a discipline for their clergy that was unknown among the sects and denominations which provided local autonomy for the congregations; Lutherans and Episcopalians were even stricter in their standards. The Southern Baptist Convention, the largest Protestant body, still permits the local congregation to ordain a minister.) Any man of serious bent and fair reputation could designate himself a preacher if he could find an empty church or meeting hall and attract a congregation: his only credential was his own word that he "felt a call to preach."

Many of these amateur gospelers preached the doctrine of "entire sanctification"—a "second blessing from the Holy Spirit" (conversion being the first), by which the redeemed man was washed clean of any innate tendency to sin, left loving only the good. Entire sanctification meant that a converted Christian didn't have to wait for death and resurrection to be absolved from his involvement in Adam's fall but might enjoy his innocence while still alive and in a happy position to testify to grace abundant.

The Methodist Church, which was the country's largest Protestant denomination until very recent years, was the first to proclaim the possibility of entire sanctification. In the Methodist Hymnal of 1905 there was a whole section of hymns devoted to "Entire Consecration and Perfect Love." One which I was

taught to sing before I was old enough to understand the words
was by no less a Methodist authority than Charles Wesley:

> O for a heart to praise my God,
> A heart from sin set free,
> A heart that always feels thy blood,
> So freely split for me.
> A heart in every thought renewed,
> And full of love divine;
> Perfect, and right, and pure, and good,
> A copy, Lord, of thine!

And that is precisely what entire sanctification meant: the recip-
ient of a second visitation from the Holy Spirit was left with a
pure heart. But when the Methodist Church rose from working
class to middle class and demanded an educated clergy, the old
doctrine was dropped, to be picked up and preserved by the
Holiness bodies, which today number a few million. I have seen
the ecstatic seizure dozens of times in brush arbors, gospel tabernacles, and churches. When the miracle of the transformation
of nature was felt, the man or woman—always many more
women than men—rose from the floor or altar rail shouting and
weeping and paraded up and down the aisles kissing everybody
within reach; when the ecstasy had exhausted itself, the happy
soul fell in a faint on a front pew.

After an absence of thirty-five years I returned to my grandparents' village church in southern Illinois. Remnants of five of
the old families remain today to support the ghost of church and
community life at the crossroads ten miles from the nearest
town. Most of them are college graduates living in modern
homes with landscaped lawns and flower gardens. The most
influential organization in the village is the garden club. The
sermon I heard in our old family church, along with about
twenty other worshipers, was a screaming tirade against the sin
of women cutting their hair. The young preacher had been entirely sanctified, and at the close of the service he pleaded long
and loud with the church members present to come to the altar

and pray for the "second blessing." Nobody moved. The gram-
mar of the sermon was as vulgar as the noisy and disorderly
service. No hymns were sung, only syncopated revivalistic
ditties.

From the same pulpit, which overlooks the beautiful churchyard and the graves of my forebears born during the Revolutionary War, my grandparents and parents listened to sermons
by gentlemen who loved the classics, wrote pious and sentimental verse as a hobby, and collected libraries on a pitiful salary.

The decline of rural and village life—my own home town
dropped from eleven hundred inhabitants in 1901 to three hundred by 1940—led of course to a decline in the level of preaching. The isolated and poorly paid pulpits, which educated
ministers could not afford to fill, became happy hunting grounds
for the crank and the bigot—the small-bore mind that has room
for only a single idea in religion and morals.

Most jackleg preachers were unsuccessful farmers; a few
were English- or Welsh-born coal miners. The British-American
miners were, however, likely to be Socialists, and their radical
sermons in the early 1900s horrified the pious farmers who were
poor men too—they were poor, but they were Republicans and
high tariff men, antilabor, anti-Catholic, and antiforeigners, particularly anti-British. They loved nothing better than to hear
their preacher twist the British lion's tail.

Brother Ansley of Hillsboro, Illinois, was a self-educated
English-born coal miner and week-end preacher who subscribed to socialist papers and distributed socialist tracts. He
lived heartily and well in a yellow and white cottage. His wife
tended two vegetable gardens and a beautiful flower garden
and kept geese and a peacock which disturbed the neighbors.

Brother Ansley had a very loud voice and he took over as song
leader at all his church services. But when he reached the burden and heat of his sermon, his cockney dialect was hard for his
American congregation to follow. His favorite text was from the
Magnificat, Mary's song of rejoicing in the first chapter of Luke:

"He hath put down the mighty from their seats, and exalted them of low degree. He hath filled the hungry with good things; and the rich he hath sent empty away." Brother Ansley interpreted the gospel text literally: in the kingdom that Jesus Christ came to establish, earthly fortunes would be exactly reversed, the first would be last and the last first; those people who had been poor and lowly would be exalted and rich, but the rich and proud who had everything in this world would suffer deprivation.

Such radical preaching was more than many of Brother Ansley's congregation could take—they were poor farmers and small businessmen, not coal miners like the minister. Sunday collections fell below five dollars and the fiery preacher had to quit.

There was the backwoods preacher in Newton County, Missouri, who made a precarious living cutting railroad ties, fence posts, and firewood; his collections from Saturday night and Sunday preaching would not have kept his pack of hound dogs alive. This man always used two spittoons, one at each end of the long low platform in his unpainted plank-on-end tabernacle, in which in winter he also stored his scanty harvest of corn, wheat, and stock peas. (Cigarette smokers who never took up tobacco chewing nor have friends who did cannot imagine the marvelous dexterity which a proud devotee might achieve spitting through a knothole or in a cat's eye. Civil War veterans, who were still around in large numbers at the turn of the century, had brought the lifetime habit home with them from the army.)

From the moment that tobacco-chewing preacher began his sermon to the end he never paused even once in his quick, jerky paces from one end of the platform to the other. Twice in each round he hitched up his trousers, first one side, then the other. The poor fellow was winded when he quit, gasping for breath, his dark blue shirt and blue denim pants black with sweat. But what fascinated older boys in the congregation was his unerring aim from between his teeth as he rounded each turn within shot of a spittoon. One of his neighbors declared that the length of the sermon was determined not by inspiration but by the size of the chew in the preacher's cheek.

I found it hard to follow a sermon delivered on the run, but I remember a few snatches, perhaps because they were original if not profound:

"Adam didn't whup his young 'uns, he let 'em run wild in the Garden with all the animals. And that's how sin and cussedness and murder got started. Oh, Adam may have whupped the stuffin's out o' them sassy boys, but he didn't whup their britches off. I whup my young 'uns ever time they needs it, and that's plenty. I hope you do too. My pa whupped me till I was old enough to court the gals. If there's one thing I cain't stand, h'its a sassy boy. . . .

"And what about Eve? What was ole Mother Eve doin' all that time? Why, she was so took up with listenin' to a snake talk she had no mind for doin' a woman's part. She had to be smarter 'n her man. That's no good. That's bad.

"That old Devil serpent, you can bet he was put in the Garden fer some purpose—God, he don't do things by guesswork, he *knows*. He had to know what he'd done when he made man and woman. He found out quick enough. H'its all here. H'its God's word. Praise the Lord!"

Forty-seven years ago a rural circuit in a border state was served by a young Southerner of limited preparation but with boundless zeal. Although he was only twenty-eight years old, Brother Finer was breaking in a full set of dentures when he conducted a "protracted meeting" in one of his three little churches. He invited me, his neighbor, to go with him to the closing service. The road through the woods and along a creek bed was so narrow and treacherous that I was afraid the old Model T would never make it to church. On the way my neighbor told me he had "cleaned the altar" four times the night before. He meant that the altar rail was filled four times with mourners and, as he put it, "everybody got through"—that is, every sinner who answered the preacher's altar call went away satisfied that he had been saved.

Brother Finer had hardly started his strenuous sermon when both his upper and lower dentures flew from his open mouth, sailed across the bare space between the altar rail and the front pew, struck the floor, and skidded to a stop under an occupied pew. The preacher was dismayed only momentarily. He left the pulpit, ran down the aisle, retrieved his false teeth on his hands and knees, wiped them with his handkerchief, returned them to place, and resumed his sermon.

The preacher's wife sat in a front pew that night because the little frame church was crowded. She had been a country school-teacher; her future husband was her oldest pupil in the last term she taught. She was not as pious as he, but was reserved, prissy. Her husband's misfortune in public was more than she could take; she refused to speak to him on the long ride back to town. The next morning my neighbor appeared at my front door, wearing the countenance of a sheep-killing dog; his wife had refused to get up and prepare breakfast and look after the two-year-old daughter.

Another Sunday night my ardent young neighbor waxed too exuberant over his success in a revival at another church and leaped too high, hit his head on a low rafter over the pulpit and was knocked unconscious.

Brother Finer served only the poorest rural circuits for thirty-odd years and died in poverty and obscurity. His emotional type of evangelism lost face in his part of the country; congregations in big cities and larger towns scorned it. My old neighbor's one talent came to a falling market, and his fortunes fell with it.

In those years, when the Grand Army of the Republic was the power structure in our national life, there were a few preachers and many politicians who aped the careless dress and slouch and earthy (just this side of the barnyard) idiom that they attributed to Abraham Lincoln, whom few if any of them had ever seen. This streak of vulgarity in the pulpit never dies out, though until very recent years it was frowned upon by church people.

For example: The minister of a large church was invited to deliver the high-school baccalaureate sermon at an industrial center which had a high proportion of college men and women. He put his capacity congregation in stitches by describing at length the gravel path bordered by pretty shells that led from the kitchen door of his boyhood home to a small white building in the back yard, and the out-of-date Sears, Roebuck catalog that hung on a nail. That preacher's own congregation included a few hundred college students and faculty members—they must have taken their Sunday worship with this man as a merry holiday from the sobriety of the intellectual community.

Another example: A lovely little brick and stone church stands a block off a major highway in one of the most attractive small towns in the Missouri Ozarks. It was filled for the morning service, and nearly every man, woman, and child in the congregation knew everybody else. Many of them were college graduates; they included schoolteachers and other professional people and several public officials; there were at least twenty-five college and high school students. The singing of the hymns, an anthem, and the choir responses were excellent under the direction of a professional musician, with a competent organist. But the sermon was a ghastly stand-in for preaching. It was a screaming tirade against all the scholars who have labored at translations of the "Old Book" since King James, and against "the godless, immoral universities and colleges and infidel-ridden seminaries."

The climax was unforgettable, and no wonder. The preacher rolled his Bible tightly in his fist and brandished it like a cudgel over his head. Then from that gladiatorial posture he named a dozen of the most renowned clergymen in the land and shouted at the top of his voice, "I'd just as soon have a big black nigger in my pul-pit!"

Now that preacher is a college graduate, without theological training. In conversation he uses perfect English, but in the pulpit for some reason he prefers the homespun vernacular from his backwoods childhood. Outside his pulpit he is the friendliest of men, generous and charitable; as a pastor he never forgets the poor and needy, the sick, the aged and shut-ins. He has a good record in recruiting new members for his churches. But he has never shed his fundamentalist Pentecostal background—he says he left his parents' denomination because there was no future in it for an ambitious young man. His racial and religious prejudices are violent, and he never misses an opportunity to challenge the liberal opposition. His favorite stump for debate is the low stone wall in front of the courthouse, with his white and tan bird dog at his feet.

This county-seat church belongs to the Methodist Church, a denomination which supports colleges and universities and theological seminaries from coast to coast. Its schools, publications of every kind, and most of its clergy are liberal. The congregation under review is dominated by the civic leaders of the little community—men and women who are outspoken liberals in religion, education, and politics. During the first decade of this century, that county had a considerable Socialist Party vote. The church draws many city visitors because the town is the shopping center of a large resort area. The old congregation has had several liberal pastors; at least three became distinguished city ministers. Denominational rivalry has kept all the town's churches small, so that able or promising ministers are not likely to accept a call to such a limited field.

I watched the response of that congregation to the sermon. There was no reaction except on the faces of some teenagers and young adults who plainly were embarrassed. The older people had come to church because it was their habit. They still come. They are not likely to lose the feeling that it is their church, not the preacher's. The local church is a hardy plant. It has absorbed a lot of abuse and punishment and neglect from friend and foe. In endurance at least, it is a Rock of Ages.

The class meeting was the Methodist institution for the care of souls in the absence of the circuit-riding minister, who brought his sermon two Sundays a month and went away with ten dollars in currency and silver, mostly silver. Men and women of the congregation stood up before their relatives and friends and neighbors and confessed their trials and temptations in biblical terms. Almost every testimonial ended in the same words, "Pray for me that I may ever be faithful."

Instituted by John Wesley, the class meeting was the fore-runner of the modern vogue of pastoral counseling, which has developed at a furious pace into a pseudoscience and is our most prevalent form of amateur psychiatry. Ministers now complain or boast of spending many times as much time on counseling as on their sermons, and more hours than on pastoral calling and the necessary business of the church. Preaching gets the fag end of the week's work.

Circuit riders of all evangelical denominations sixty years ago counseled scores of troubled persons in the course of a year. The old-time counselor followed a standard routine: he first listened, then read verses from the Bible that seemed to him to apply, and closed the session with prayer. His prayer was very personal; it spoke of "thy servant here," and often used the first name. The counselor was strictly on his own. Even if he was a seminary graduate, he had never heard of courses in pastoral counseling; he did not have access to a library on the subject.

One day in 1903, a class meeting was in progress in a one-room country church. It lasted an hour, and about half the people who had attended the earlier Sunday school remained. The wallpapered sanctuary, with rag carpet on the pulpit plat-form and in the two aisles, was heated by two big wood and coal stoves, one against the north wall and the other exactly opposite inside the south aisle. There was no cloakroom so we stacked our heavy coats in empty pews. The big room was pleasantly filled with the odor of fresh stove polish that the fires heated and made to shine.

The meeting was conducted with great dignity by an old

farmer who was also superintendent of the Sunday school. He quoted Bible verses now and then and generally spoke a few words of encouragement to the man or woman who had just stood up and given testimony. More women than men spoke up, but then as now there were more women in church. Farm women led lonelier lives, too, and they must have derived sound relief from speaking up. Often when they had finished they sat down and wept. The service was a lay activity, not at all like a confessional; there were vague and pious confessions but no penance.

What I most vividly remember about those old exercises in mutual aid is their sorrowful tone. The faces of the men and women were sad, and there was much weeping. They talked about sickness and death and heaven. In contrast, public worship nowadays is a feast of merriment. Christians now shun the word death as though it were impious and in bad taste and substitute "passed away." Sixty years ago little children were taken to funerals and held up so they might look at the face in the casket.

When the class meeting played out for lack of volunteers, a favorite Fanny Crosby hymn was sung to a slow reed organ accompaniment:

> Blessed assurance! Jesus is mine,
> Oh, what a foretaste of glory divine.
> Heir of salvation, purchase of God,
> Born of His Spirit, washed in His blood.

That stanza perfectly expresses evangelical faith and preaching at the turn of the century. Fanny Crosby's ninety-five years, 1820 to 1915, spanned almost exactly the era of the rise and spread of evangelical Protestantism. Blind from infancy, she wrote eight thousand gospel songs. A few of the others which my generation could sing without the book were: "Pass me not, O gentle Saviour, Hear my humble cry; While on others thou art calling, Do not pass me by"; "Thou my everlasting portion, More than friend or life to me, All along my pilgrim journey, Saviour, let me walk with thee"; "Every day, every hour, Let me feel thy cleansing power; May thy tender love to me, Bind me closer, closer, Lord, to thee"; "Rescue the perishing, Care for the dying; Jesus is merciful, Jesus will save." The favorite hymn of all evangelical Protestants was, however, Charles Wesley's "Jesus, Lover of my soul."

Religion was intensely personal and subjective—like those gospel songs, like the class meeting and pastoral care. Those earlier congregations were converts from revival meetings and from altar calls at the climax of Sunday worship. Conversion was an emotional experience and unreflective. The convert had felt the Spirit moving him; he knew his sinful nature had been "washed in the blood of the Lamb." He was not expected to explain the mystery.

Sermons of the time were highly emotional, too, even from the educated clergy. They were theologically barren; they were moralistic, practical. A single sermon might bring in Noah's ark, Lot's wife, and the sin of Sunday train excursions.

The preacher's subject one Sunday morning was the believer's trust in God, his text the Twenty-third Psalm. After disposing of his scripture in a couple of minutes, the preacher shouted and whispered and ranted and wept and mopped his face for nearly an hour. He took at least a fourth of the time to tell an intimate story brought to the pulpit from the bosom of his own family.

The preacher had a daughter three years old who was uncommonly timid by nature. She fled to her mother's arms from any visitor who tried to make friends. Her father was anxious to give his child more confidence in herself and in other people. One day he tried something new and was overjoyed when it worked. He led the child to a thick post that supported the mailbox at the front gate and set her on top. After a round of coddling talk he told the child to let go of the post and leap into his arms; he would catch her and it would be fun. When the preacher repeated over and over to the congregation the plea he made to his child, "Come to papa! Come to papa!" tears streamed down his cheeks.

In the past ten years, however, I have not heard this weepy kind of preaching in churches as often as I did many years ago, but the Lord only knows how many times I have heard it on radio. It never dies out.

# 2

# When Preaching
# Was in Favor and Flower

The zenith of American Protestant preaching lasted fifty years—
from about 1880 to the Great Depression. The pulpit has not
enjoyed the same prestige since. The churches have had to make
the painful adjustment to minority status in a mushrooming
national population.

The postwar boom in church construction, membership, and
attendance from 1946 through the late fifties was not really a
happy time for the clergy. They were more troubled than elated
—it looked too much like another Mississippi Bubble or wild-
catting in oil. As one veteran pastor put it, "I'm glad my retirement is at hand. My church is spending forty-five thousand dollars for a new pipe organ when the inner-city missions of our
denomination are starving."

It was not thus in the good old days from Garfield to Hoover.
By 1880 the national slump in morals and religion that followed
the Civil War had ebbed and churches had found their second
wind. The upper middle class was prospering, which meant
good times for Protestantism. The goose hung high in the Gilded
Age. By the turn of the century the carriage-trade churches were
supremely confident in their prosperity and self-esteem. They
embraced the people who counted. Their total membership was
outnumbered several times by the non-Protestant masses, but

this was accepted as a mark of distinction—the Lord must know
his own.

A church deacon could be spotted a block away. He appeared
at five minutes to eleven wearing a morning coat, striped gray
trousers, and mouse-colored spats, boutonniere, top hat and
gloves, and swinging a cane. His social standing was measured
by the number of times he was called by his first name. He was
shown to his reserved pew and handed his hymnbook and
printed order of worship with the same deference he received
at a symphony concert or first-night theater. The length of the
sermon was what gave the good man the comfortable feeling
that he was setting a good example and doing his duty to God
and country so the Lord would forgive him for any shenanigans
he might engage in downtown during the coming week.

A United States senator and Presbyterian ruling elder was as
familiar a figure on St. Louis' Union Boulevard as the carved
stone hitching posts and the horse blocks. On Sunday mornings
he represented the social register families whose three-story
dwellings lined the exclusive residential places guarded at each
end by stone turrets and iron gates. The wealthiest Presbyterian
church in the first quarter of the century faced a lovely little
public park which today is not safe to enter after dark; the big
stone church has been a Pentecostal center for a generation.
Two governors of Illinois and one of Missouri were cocks of the
walk in their Methodist churches.

The clergy of the elect were the chaplains of the middle class,
which was on the make. Their social standing was secure and
high. They were community personages, listened to with respect, showered with favors: babies were named for them. At
the dinner table, people talked about their preacher and his
sermons as they might discuss fashions and foods and politics
and the children's future. Walter Reuther, president of the
United Automobile Workers, says that when he was a little boy
growing up in a devout Lutheran household, he and his brother
were sharply quizzed by their father at Sunday dinner on the
points which their preacher had made in his long sermon—"and

we had better know the answers if we expected to be let out of
the house to play."

A new church could be built for a hundred thousand dollars
in the shape of an opera house, the pulpit and choir taking the
place of the proscenium and stage—the exalted place of the
pulpit was the determining factor. Sunday schools, Christian
Endeavor, the Epworth League, and foreign missions flourished.
Temples of worship occupied choice corners on the boulevards.
And it was a rare village that couldn't boast of at least five rival
congregations—the trick was to snare a substantial family of
newcomers before its furnishings were unpacked.

Before the end of the happy era the Pentecostal sects and
store-front chapels of the poor were getting started. In their
tabernacles, unlike churches of the Establishment, the deacons
were both men and women; the men appeared in shirtsleeves
and the women in house dresses; their preacher was probably
a streetcar operator or barber or laborer during the week.

The Pentecostals are the only major religious movement to
appear in this century, and they stand wholly apart from the
rest of the Christian structure. This ecstatic movement arose in
the first decade, took a tremendous spurt during the Depression
years when Protestantism was sharply divided along social lines
and ideologically blurred, and today possibly numbers some
four or five millions in the United States in dozens of branches,
which makes total membership difficult to assess.

The first Pentecostal meeting I attended was in a preaching
shed (an abandoned store) in a coal-mining town in southern
Illinois more than fifty years ago. All I remember was the
speaking in unknown tongues, mostly by women, several taking
part at the same time. To the habitual churchgoer, the jabber-
wocky was appalling, not amusing. There was nothing in the
seizures to suggest an invasion from heaven.

Forty years later I covered a national Pentecostal convention
in St. Louis, and the friendly, pretty, and stylishly dressed
young woman at the reception desk said to me, "I don't like to

remind you that you will hear speaking in tongues at our worship sessions, for you will think it is all we stand for. It is only one manifestation of the Holy Spirit. What we get in our religion is all the gifts of the Spirit—rebirth and sanctification. So please pay attention to the convention reports on our high schools and colleges and theological seminaries and hospitals. We are very proud of our medical missions. The Pentecostal Publishing House is one of the largest of its kind in the country."

But in the happy era of Protestant preaching, the noisy presence of these new congregations without lineage was accepted by the quality folk with equanimity. It was obvious anyway that their adherents would be limited to the poor, who just might respond to their uneducated ministry and stay away from the august oak and brass doors, keeping their proper place in society. The fervent preaching they heard of the Second Coming of the Lord—a neglected doctrine in a world that already appeared to be the best possible—would not only save those poor souls, a mission hitherto assigned to the Salvation Army; it might well be expected further to chasten their behavior under the hardships which Providence laid upon them.

There were other small clouds on the Protestant horizon, but not bigger than a man's hand. The Roman Catholics were throwing their weight of numbers around in politics, but in religion still kept to their Latinized ghetto. Jews were blackballed in high society and barred from the best clubs and the fashionable residential areas where the largest Protestant congregations gathered. But Jews could not be ignored in business and the professions and the entertainment world. Louis D. Brandeis attained to the Supreme Court. Negroes were migrating to the cities faster than they were needed for the dirty work.

The old-line churches were changing, too, under social pressures. The substantial Protestant layman still appeared in style on Sunday morning, but he had quit reading his Bible at home, dropped family prayer and table grace, and no longer found it convenient to serve Sunday chicken to his minister. But this layman knew what he believed on Sunday, and his pastor had better know what his layman believed too. A typical sermon sounded like a sound, solid editorial in the morning newspaper. There was a happy marriage of pulpit and pew.

It was wonderful to be living in those Theodore Roosevelt– William Jennings Bryan–Andrew Mellon years. It was the last go-around for a Protestant-ruled world that was about to be shattered forever.

At historic First Congregational (Unitarian) Church in Cambridge, directly across the street from the Harvard College gates, on an average Sunday morning during the academic year, included in the small congregation in box stalls were only two young men from the Yard, both divinity school students. A few blocks away, in the crowded Roman Catholic cathedral, hundreds of students were at mass, and the sermon they heard was a scathing denunciation of almost everything they were taught in their Harvard classes. Thus their parents provided their sons with the best of both worlds—a Protestant education and the family tradition of Catholic faith and Catholic marriage.

At Old South Church in Boston, another Congregational preacher, friend of governors and Harvard presidents, was rallying the saints for a procession that had already passed them by. George A. Gordon was the last of the "Proper Bostonian" pulpiteers, straight out of the Victorian age and the autumnal years of Protestant rhetoric and Adam Smith. He preached twice every Sunday—for many years now most of the clergy and laity of his genteel world have closed their engagement with God by noon. Gordon was preaching from what another Bostonian, Justice Oliver Wendell Holmes, called a "protected cloister" when Sacco and Vanzetti were on their slow march to the electric chair. Today his published sermons are curiously dated. At national church conventions at Chicago, Houston, Miami Beach, and Kansas City, I have asked groups of young ministers if they ever read his books; not one has, and only two or three out of a hundred even know his name. Gordon's majestic affirmations of faith in God in the face of evil and the triumph of righteousness just do not go down anymore in a world that has witnessed the horrors of Buchenwald and Hiroshima.

Gordon's preaching is recalled not to criticize a man for being a child of his time and social class but to show what has happened to his calling in the past half century. The old-fashioned sonority of the pulpit six feet above reply is dead and buried beyond resurrection. Preachers are more on their own today than at any time since Martin Luther and John Calvin.

The patricians' *noblesse oblige* version of Christianity has virtually disappeared. The Unitarian movement almost died from this dry rot. In that gilded age from McKinley through Coolidge, the Unitarian preacher was expected to dismiss good-humoredly Adam and Eve and the axe that swam and Jonah and the whale. But it was as good as his neck if he sounded like Samuel Gompers or dropped as much as a hint that the Polish and Irish domestics in the households of his constituents might aspire to the God-pleasing precincts of the Mayflower Society.

A Congregational colleague of Boston's George Gordon was Samuel Woodrow. He was a cousin of President Woodrow Wilson but a stanch Republican of Mark Hanna coloration. He was pastor of Pilgrim Congregational Church in St. Louis, one of the largest congregations in the city and known as the "Cathedral of Congregationalism" in the Middle West. During Woodrow's pastorate and for years afterward, this church gave more money to foreign missions than any other church in the denomination.

Woodrow, a huge man and an imposing figure in his pulpit, was one of the two or three most quoted clergymen in the city. It was 1916, and an eyelash-finish national election (Wilson versus Charles Evans Hughes) was heating up the war-stoked prosperous domestic scene. Congress was driven by President Wilson to pass the Adamson Act, establishing the eight-hour day for railway workers engaged in interstate transportation. As the proper subject for a fire-eating, labor-baiting sermon from an upper-class Protestant pulpit like Woodrow's, it was almost too good to be true. As church news reporter for the old *St.*

*Louis Star,* I covered the service in Pilgrim Church and wrote a full column on the sermon. The "color" in my story included Woodrow's scathing denunciation of Congress for bowing to the will of the President on "the pregnant hinges of the knee." After the service it was a happy scene as the proud worshipers crowded around their minister to congratulate him.

Monday morning a storm broke over my head. My managing editor, Frank W. Taylor, Jr., a Catholic, called me to his desk in a rage. He threatened to fire me for using the word "pregnant" in a story for a family newspaper. When I explained that Woodrow was quoting Shakespeare, it added insult to outrage. But my column, with the preacher's language scrubbed up, appeared.

A few blocks from Pilgrim Church was another fashionable church of equal wealth and social standing. During the years of this congregation's most flourishing growth and property-building its pastor was another patrician. Dr. Blank spoke no evil, heard no evil, saw no evil. His favorite sermon illustrations were the dew on the grass, birds in the trees, the beauty and glory of God's world. He never saw the slums which crept within three blocks of his elegant church or the lines of thousands of unemployed. It was always moonlight and roses for his Sunday morning faith. American boys, St. Louis boys, were literally coughing up their lungs rotted by poison gas in the trenches overseas; many of their families were on public relief. But were not the magnolia trees and lilacs blooming in the yards of the marble palaces along Lindell Boulevard? God was in his heaven, all was right in his world.

Twenty years later, a labor-management forum was held by the churchmen's club in Dr. Blank's church. Some seventy laymen, including several big names from the industrial and financial world, attended the dinner meeting. The spokesman for management was an officer of the Missouri Chamber of Commerce. The views he expressed in his opening statement were so reactionary and labor-hating that they would have been repudiated by the St. Louis Chamber; the state Chamber represented

small industrial plants located in small towns in order to escape
labor unions and their wage scales. But this man knew his
church audience; those men made him feel right at home, he
"belonged to the club." Most of his speech was in support of
right-to-work laws which ban the union shop. His own state,
Missouri, has no such law.

The spokesman for labor was an executive officer of the CIO,
a moderate, mild-mannered liberal reared in the old Evangelical
Synod (German Reformed). In his opening statement he cited
the gains which the organized labor movement had brought to
millions of American families, in income, housing, opportunities
for education, diet and health, and recreation. He also defended
the right of churches and clergy and the National Council of
Churches to speak out on public issues that involved human
welfare.

After the two opening statements, there was a question-and-
answer period. This continued for an hour and a half, until the
minister, embarrassed by the one-sided affair, called it a day.
In those ninety minutes, not one question was addressed to the
representative of management. But the labor representative was
pelted with questions—all of them hostile or loaded, not a few
malicious and insulting. "What are you doing about the Communists in your labor unions?" "When are you going to clean
house of the labor racketeers and other criminal elements?"
"What makes you fellows think you know more about running
the plant than management?" "I suppose you think it is all right
for John L. Lewis to call a strike of his coal miners in wartime
when patriotic Americans are dying in battle?" "Are you union
leaders prepared to drag this country all the way into collec-
tivism?" And so on. Not once did the labor spokesman lose his
temper, not even when the question was framed to give the
impression that the answer was going to be a lie.

After the meeting, I asked the labor council man, an old
friend, to take me home. "Oscar," I asked, "why do you submit
to such abuse as you took tonight? Why do you accept invita-

tions to address church forums when you know in advance the crowd will be opposed to everything you stand for?"

"I feel that I have to; it is part of my public relations job. The laymen are nearly always worse than the clergy. Many of the clergy are good friends of organized labor—they face opposition, too."

That labor-management forum in a patrician church where one side was feted and the other thrown to the wolves came back to mind on two other occasions—in 1956, from the minister of a large suburban congregation: "My church is fortunate, we have no labor." In 1962, from the popular pastor of one of the largest and fastest-growing churches in a large metropolitan area: "My heart goes out to all my good men who must spend days and nights negotiating contracts with those labor-union men."

# 3

# The Rebels Storm
# the Patrician Heaven

The church Establishment and the patrician preachers had their high, wide, and handsome way for fifty years. Almost, that is, but not quite. Midway in their complacent reign, when World War I was in the offing, rebels appeared at the barricades and stormed the gates of the Protestant heaven. These disturbers of the peace came bringing a fighting version of the Judaeo-Christian faith that has been known ever since as the Social Gospel. While it lasted, the struggle between the traditionalists and the reformers was the most exciting chapter in American church history until the Negro revolution of the 1950s.

At about the time Woodrow Wilson was first elected President on his New Freedom reform platform, I was program chairman of the Epworth League of Union Methodist Episcopal Church (Northern) in St. Louis. This group of teenagers and young adults met on Sunday evening at six for a snack, followed by a meeting for worship and study. Our sponsor was the handsome and popular minister, a liberal who violated the Northern Methodist antitobacco law for preachers by smoking cigars on the sly. We were studying the famous Social Creed of Methodism which had been adopted by the Baltimore General Conference of 1908:

"The Methodist Episcopal Church stands:

"For the gradual and reasonable reduction of the hours of labor to the lowest practical point, with work for all; and for that degree of leisure for all which is the condition of the highest human life.

"For the highest wage that each industry can afford, and for the most equitable division of the products of industry that can ultimately be devised."*

Our big St. Louis congregation was fertile soil for the roots of the new reform movement. It was a cross section of the city's white Protestant life—from ten-dollar-a-week clerks to millionaires. It was inevitable that we should divide over the social creed of our denomination, as happened in most Protestant churches. Our beloved Union Church minister, then in vigorous middle life, was a supporter of the 1908 Social Creed, but his rich laymen were definitely hostile. The minister knew, and gave discreet approval, that our Epworth League group received outside help in its research and study in social problems.

About half a dozen of us had met Harry F. Ward, secretary of the Methodist Federation for Social Service, who gave us lists of books and periodicals to read; we had also heard him speak at several church conferences. Ward was a tall, slender, ascetic-looking man with a large head; his speech delivery was cool and professorial; he argued for the most far-reaching social reforms in the tone of voice of a man ordering coffee and doughnuts at a lunch counter.

A few years later, when I was a preministerial student at McKendree College in Lebanon, Illinois, a Methodist school, I renewed acquaintances with several members of my old Ep-

* By 1948 the Methodist Church—since 1939 a reunion of the Northern with the more conservative Southern branch of Methodism—had homogenized its Social Creed to read, in part: "We stand for reasonable hours of labor, for just wages, for a fair day's work for a fair day's wage, for fair working conditions, for periods of leisure for those who work, and for an equitable division of the product of industry."

worth League group at a meeting in St. Louis where Ward was
the speaker. World War I was a ghastly blood-letting in Europe,
and at home President Wilson's policy of "benevolent neutral-
ity" was coming under increasing fire from former President
Theodore Roosevelt and other Republican leaders. Ward talked
to us young churchmen about the danger of United States entry
into the war. His opinion was that we would fight, and he
warned us of the pressures for conformity which war would
bring; social reforms would be assailed by its inveterate enemies
as unpatriotic.

It was before the war came to America that our study group
in Union Church ran into stormy weather. We were the not so
innocent cause of a split in the congregation. We knew we had
both our minister and many sympathizers on our side. But a
wealthy shoe manufacturer from the congregation heard that
we were studying socialism. He appeared unexpectedly with
our minister one Sunday evening—he was the maddest man I
have ever seen. When he left, our minister informed us sadly
that our study of the Social Creed of Methodism must stop—
"Mr. Brown says there will be no socialism in Union Church."
And that was that.

But the Social Gospel and the Methodist social creed had a
stout champion in a higher place than Harry F. Ward and his
associates. Bishop Francis J. McConnell, of the Methodist
Church area of Pittsburgh, Pennsylvania, served as bishop from
1912 to 1944—the tempestuous years of the Social Gospel movement. McConnell had great personal prestige as well as courage; he had been president of DePauw University; he was an
equally attractive personality in the pulpit and in debate from
the floor—witty, urbane, and a master of language. A public
figure in his industrial parish, and beloved of newspapermen,
he was on the firing line for being a forceful spokesman for the
rights of labor. He had a large part in writing the 1919 report
on the steel strike for the Interchurch World Movement, a
documentary report that was given credit for influence in the

abolition of the twelve-hour-day and seven-day week in the steel industry.

Bishop McConnell was at the peak of his influence in the 1930s when the steel and automobile workers were organized by the new Congress of Industrial Organizations. He expounded his Social Gospel views in sermons and addresses, books and articles, in Methodist Church conferences, in the Methodist House of Bishops which was divided over the issue, and in the Federal Council of Churches.

At several Methodist conferences, I heard two characteristic stories of Bishop McConnell's charm and *modus operandi.* When the steel workers were on strike, he had a face-to-face encounter with Charles M. Schwab, president of Bethlehem Steel Company and a former president of the United States Steel Corporation. The scholarly bishop corrected Schwab on statistics of the industry which the steel executive quoted; and McConnell demonstrated that he knew more about wages and hours and working conditions—and profits—than Schwab. The other story concerns a wealthy Methodist layman of Pittsburgh who was asked by a colleague in the steel industry why he "put up with a radical Socialist" like Bishop McConnell. "I'm not going to leave my church because my bishop is a damned fool," the layman replied.

Another shining light of the Social Gospel in its heyday (afterward its sharpest critic) was Reinhold Niebuhr, who walked labor's picket lines in sympathy, then became the most famous American theologian since Jonathan Edwards. He was born in an Evangelical Synod manse in a small town on the western edge of St. Louis and grew up in the synod when it was still a German-language enclave. After receiving the conservative education which the synod provided in college and theological seminary, Niebuhr served as pastor of Bethel Evangelical Church in Detroit from 1915 to 1928. Many of his parishioners were employed in the automobile plants, and Niebuhr was shocked by the poverty and squalor in which workers and

their families lived in the motor capital of the world. He sided
with the workers in their long struggle to organize the industry
and win favorable union contracts. At Bethel Church, Niebuhr
was assisted by several young vicars, senior students from the
theological seminaries of the Evangelical Synod, and he was
able to show them the facts of life in the workingman's world.
Some of his assistants became lifetime Social Gospelers.

In those turbulent years, Niebuhr and his colleagues in the
Social Gospel movement called themselves Christian socialists.
(At McKendree College, my band of congenial spirits chose
the same banner—we had never heard of either Reinhold Niebuhr or Karl Marx.) In 1928 Niebuhr left Detroit for New York,
to join the faculty of Union Theological Seminary, which was
then a rallying ground for Christian socialists and, even further
to the left, men who united Christian theology and piety with
Marxist social and economic doctrines.

Niebuhr moved away from the Social Gospel onto the
Himalayan heights of theology; he became the most effective
critic of the sentimental optimism which infected Protestant
thought and church life in the prewar period. Niebuhr became
a byword for a new theology that scorned all trust in man's
goodness of nature and turned instead to the grace of God as
his only hope of salvation. He was a prolific writer, and for
nearly twenty years his books were the law and the gospel in
many theological seminaries of the liberal tradition. Such books
as *Beyond Tragedy* and *The Nature and Destiny of Man*—at
first glance shocking in their pessimism to a naïve, hopeful
generation of do-gooders—engaged Protestant thought and
preaching. The Social Gospel never recovered from the assaults
of Niebuhr's modern version of Calvinism—the fallen nature
of man and the absolute sovereignty of God—which formed a
penetrating critique of liberal optimism.

My generation of Christian eager beavers got more fun and
excitement from the debates over the Social Gospel than from
lectures on the evils of liquor and tobacco or from packing
missionary barrels with castoff clothing and housewares; no

churchgoers have had as much fun since. Back in my Epworth League days, we took a Broadway trolley to a public park in Carondelet to hear Eugene V. Debs, candidate for President of the Socialist Party. Debs looked like a country preacher, but he was a superb soapbox orator; his voice ranged from biting scorn for the privileged classes to sweetness and light as he described the sufferings and nobility of the poor. We Methodist liberals recognized Debs's positive demands as being our own. Since from the age of fifteen I had been reading Walter Rauschenbusch, the bright morning star of the Social Gospel movement, I could hardly forget our aims and hopes: in 1908 these included graduated federal income and inheritance taxes, government-sponsored medical care for all persons unable to pay, unemployment insurance, old-age pensions, a shorter work week, paid vacations, laws to protect women and children, decent housing for the poor and the lower middle class, federal aid to education, municipally owned public utilities, development of public parks and playgrounds where they were needed most, guaranteed rights of labor to organize and strike, fair play for minority groups, and antitrust laws.

On our way home from the Debs meeting, my crowd argued whether our future as social reformers lay in the Socialist Party or the Methodist Church.

Early in the 1930s, when the Depression was at its worst, Norman Thomas, another perennial Socialist candidate for President, visited the southeast Missouri Lead Belt where the payroll of the Work Projects Administration exceeded the local industrial payroll. Thomas had left the Presbyterian ministry to lead the Socialist Party. He was invited to the Lead Belt by an informal group of ministers and public-school administrators and teachers. Despite a heavy snowstorm that made highways almost impassable, Thomas spoke to a standing room only crowd in a large Methodist church. Ten years later, no such group of sponsors could have been found for a Norman Thomas appearance.

The liberal forces from the churches—the Social Gospelers—

put up their hardest and most successful fight during the Depression. These churchmen looked upon the soup kitchens,
many of them church-sponsored, as a national disgrace. They
were outraged by the sight of men, women, and children standing in line for handouts. The minister of the largest church in
his town told me he got up at four o'clock to start the fire under
the community kettle in which gallons of soup were prepared,
but that he never arrived on the scene without finding someone
waiting.

Another minister in a Middle West industrial community
was rebuilding his parsonage, and the foreman on the job advertised for an extra laborer to push wheelbarrow loads of brick
and mortar. The next morning before daylight, thirty-six unemployed men were milling about in the parsonage yard waiting
to apply for the job. One was hired and thirty-five turned away;
the minister saw a dozen men weeping as they left his churchyard. At the same time, industrial executives and other businessmen and their wives from his congregation were insisting
to this liberal minister that the only unemployed were the no-
goods who didn't really want jobs, who preferred to live on the
public dole.

What the liberal clergy and their supporters from the laity
demanded and, in most places, won, were measures of relief
less degrading than soup kitchens, rummage sales, and free
flour distributed by the American Red Cross disaster relief.

Truman B. Douglass was pastor of Pilgrim Congregational
Church in St. Louis from 1936 to 1943—this was Samuel Woodrow's pulpit in 1916. Douglass now is executive vice president
of the United Church Board for Homeland Ministries. At Pilgrim Church one Sunday morning, as the congregation filed
out, they were startled to see a small table in the narthex. It
held a few items of the plainest food—beans, a few potatoes, a
bowl of flour, not much else. Most conspicuous was a large
poster: "This is what the families on relief will have for Sunday
dinner. What will you have?"

At the bottom of the Depression, Truman Douglass was the

head of a team of five Congregational ministers that led a conference of church youth at Drury College in Springfield, Missouri. He had already established himself as spokesman of the liberal clergy of his denomination in Missouri. Sessions of the youth conference included chapel talks, informal discussions between students and members of the clergy team, individual conferences, and bull sessions of the team at late hours when the students were supposed to be in bed.

Douglass was exceedingly popular with the students, many of whom were having a hard time staying in college and paying the modest fees. His appeal for the serious-minded young people was many sided. To begin with, he understood their practical problems, and was a most articulate apostle of social reforms in which his young listeners had a real concern. (Douglass took a Master's degree in sociology before he decided to enter the ministry, in which his family had long been distinguished.) In religion—and more than half of his conference talks were on this subject—he was more liberal in theology than nearly all the churches from which the Drury College students came. He was also a most personable minister, a superb storyteller, widely traveled and widely read—a delightful companion and mentor to the earnest young men and women who packed his conference sessions and plied him with questions. He was an accomplished violinist and once played in Abe Lyman's dance band, and at our Springfield conference he delighted everybody with his familiarity with both church hymns and popular music.

But what other clergy members of his team remember most gratefully was a coffee and doughnuts session very late one night, and far into the night, in Douglass' big first-floor room in the men's dormitory. The down-to-earth talk settled quickly on the role of church and clergy in the mounting struggle for adequate relief for the unemployed and for long-term measures to prevent such economic disaster. Three of the ministers present were under heavy fire in their churches for their liberal views. Douglass fascinated his brethren by his eloquent sum-

ming up of the night's debate; his appeal was to reason
and courage, knowledge and faith. After more than thirty years,
his encouragement is fresh and stimulating in a grateful
memory.

"The liberal minister," he said (I quote from memory), "must
expect to be attacked in a time of national crisis. He must prepare to meet attacks fair and foul. He must meet them and
answer them without losing either his head or his heart. This
means that the minister must know what he is talking about.
If he is going to talk about the hardships of unemployment, he
must know the facts of unemployment and relief. The liberal
minister is one man who can't afford to display any ignorance
of the facts. When he demands political action for social relief
and reform, he must know who is responsible for such action,
where it must come from, and how to build popular support
for change and reform. The liberal clergy must let the politicians know we hold them responsible for public welfare, that
we are watching them, and we mean business. If the attacks
we draw surprise us, so will some of the support—it has to be
aroused and mobilized.

"Attacks on the liberal minister come from many places," he
continued. "The worst of them are disguised. I have a friend
who is being criticized for his theology, but he knows the hidden motive is his leadership in organizing cooperatives for the
unemployed. The fundamentalists never overlook an opportunity to attack the liberal clergy; we must expect this, be
prepared to meet it, try to smoke it out."

Pausing for a moment to survey his intent listeners, he added
as a warning:

"Of course there are always the vested interests that oppose
any change—they are better organized than churches and ministers. We must have the facts to meet their arguments too."

No narrow advocate of causes for causes' sake, Douglass
always retained a strong sense of pastoral responsibility.

"In all this, the liberal minister must not neglect his church duties. This is terribly important. In a time of crisis, this simply means he must work longer hours than anybody else in his church. We are making progress, and we will make more."

The liberal clergy such as Douglass—Protestant, Catholic, Jew—would settle for nothing less than public work for the unemployed, immediate provision for needy persons in cash and commodity, public health services, classes in adult education to train the unemployed for opportunity when it came, the organization of labor in order that workers with jobs might win security for themselves, and cooperative projects in which unemployed men and women could produce food and clothing and household goods for themselves.

The ranks of the Social Gospel movement began to splinter during the late 1930s. Some of the leaders felt that their demands were being met by the New Deal. For some, the church-sponsored movement became identified with Marxism to the extent that it sounded like an apology for communism. For others—and their numbers have been growing ever since—the Social Gospel faith was bound up with pacifism. And of course for a larger number the movement lost its glamour, and they returned to the status quo.

Harry F. Ward was one of five ministers who organized the Methodist Federation for Social Service in 1907. He became secretary of the organization which, in time, was recognized by the Methodist General Conference as an authorized agency of the church. Later, the federation was disowned and was compelled to continue operations as an independent group. The Methodist Church went all out for prohibition and had no time or patience for other reforms. In the McCarthy period, Ward came under fire for his alleged Communist connections. Now in his nineties and living in honored retirement in New York, Ward is a hardy survivor of the Red scare and investigations by the House Committee on Un-American Activities.

Yet despite the splintering, feuding, and defections among the champions of the Social Gospel's heyday, its underlying message had penetrated church life and preaching, and remains there. Nine out of ten Methodist bishops swallow the social views of their Bishop McConnell with their morning coffee. We hear the Social Gospel preached in churches and cathedrals, by the popes of the Roman Catholic Church with vigor and unmistakable application, in college chapels, by the United Churchmen and United Church Women (who deserve a special citation here), at assemblies of the National Council of Churches and the World Council of Churches, state and local councils of churches, and by presidents of the United States, kings, queens, and prime ministers.

I covered the 1954 meeting of the Southern Baptist Convention in St. Louis—this was only weeks after the historic decision of the United States Supreme Court outlawing racial segregation in the public schools. I was at the press table when the following resolution came to a vote before the convention: "This Supreme Court decision is in harmony with the constitutional guarantees of equal freedom to all citizens, and with the Christian principles of equal justice and love for all men." The resolution further called upon all Southern Baptists "to conduct themselves in this period of adjustment in the spirit of Christ."

A vice president of the convention, a St. Louis pastor, invited me to join him on the platform while he checked the tallies of votes turned in by ushers stationed throughout the auditorium. There were some eight thousand voting delegates (messengers, they were called), and more than two thousand visitors. The convention officer and I counted fewer than twenty Nay votes. Of course there were more delegates opposed, but they were so few in number and the favorable sentiment of the convention so overwhelming that they chose not to stand and be counted. When the vote was announced, there were thunderous cheers.

During the next few years, at every annual meeting of the Southern Baptist Convention, a minority sought to overturn the

1954 resolution. They got nowhere; the stand of our largest Protestant denomination has remained unchanged.

At one of the last national church conventions I covered, the 1962 General Assembly of the United Presbyterian Church, U.S.A., a big issue on the agenda was Medicare—a proposal for government-sponsored medical care for individuals and families on Social Security. I saw delegates, clergy and lay, being buttonholed by lobbyists for the American Medical Association seeking to block any favorable action on the medical care resolution. Several delegates told me they were contacted by physicians from the convention city, Denver, who had, in turn, been contacted by physicians who belonged to the delegates' churches back home. The Presbyterian assembly took no action on medical care.

The change in the message of the churches has been in emphasis and spirit, not in principle. The pioneers of the Social Gospel were beguiled by the same naïve optimism and extravagant hopes as the conservative foreign missionary boards, who were confident that the world could be won for Christ in a single generation. In the same fine first rapture of spirit, so incredible today, the Social Gospelers actually believed they were going to build the New Jerusalem in a lifetime. It took a world revolution and a fearful shrinkage in the white man's dominion to calm them down.

The Social Gospel lost its identity but not its influence: it was one of the historic movements of the human spirit that found its life by losing it. On the negative side, it was a reaction against the patricians and their Establishment. On the positive side, it was the involvement of the church and clergy in the universal march of freedom. When Charles Howard Hopkins wrote his definitive book in 1940, *The Rise of the Social Gospel in American Protestantism,* he set its dates as 1865–1915. But he shows that the roots of the Liberal movement go back to the first quarter of the nineteenth century. Hopkins' conclusion, his very last sentence, is: "The social gospel has become an integral part of the thought and action of the Church."

As a church-news editor I heard more sermons on the Social Gospel during my last three years of active duty, 1959–1962, than in my first three years, 1914–1917. The difference was that in those last years the Social Gospel was not labeled, not dragged in as something extra and new; it was taken for granted.

Yet the Social Gospel no longer finds its finest expression in Sunday-morning sermons to the comfortable. It may be seen in shirt sleeves and white uniforms—no spats—in loving care for the aged and the very young; professional aid for handicapped children, the mentally troubled, the lonely and the forgotten in cities and towns and rural areas; on college campuses and military installations around the world; at lonely mission posts, digging latrines in the Near East and doctoring leprosy sufferers in Africa; at feeding stations in Hong Kong, and in gaslit coffee houses in American cities where the beatniks flee the responsibilities of life; at Congressional hearings where the lobbyists of vested interests drown out the voice of the people; on Indian reservations, and on the playgrounds of high-rise housing projects; counseling married couples from split-level houses, and giving vaccinations and vitamins in India; going to jail for demonstrating in behalf of human rights —and the Bill of Rights; in cancer hospitals, on Florida beaches; wherever in the world people are found hungry, or thirsty, or a stranger, or naked, or sick, or in prison.

# 4

# The Hallelujah Faith
# and Foreign Missions

A churchgoer born before the turn of the century grew up under
preaching that rang like the bells of glory land with the "Hallelujah Chorus": "Hallelujah! the kingdom of this world is become the Kingdom of our Lord and of His Christ." Notice the
jubilant tense of Handel's verb—"is become." It was thrilling.
But it was a pathetic fallacy.

The surrender of the Cross and Crown as the symbols of
ultimate Christian dominion was the biggest thing that happened to the church posture and faith and its preaching between 1910 and 1965. The shift in the Christian temper from
assumed superiority to humility was the inner side of the decline of the West. It was traumatic for the Christian army to
have to give up its dream of universal sway. But just listen to
preaching today; it is muted. It is humble, brotherly, compas-
sionate. It is sober with penitence, beautiful for comradeship.
It is not the Master's voice that speaks but a servant's.

What is revolutionary in the change is the new attitude
toward mankind's other religions: Christians now not only
treat them with respect but acknowledge their rightful place
in the scheme of things. To take the most famous example,
Western Christians today freely confess that it would be ludi-
crous to call Mahatma Gandhi a "heathen in his blindness

bowing down to wood and stone," for Gandhi was a man whose vision of human unity had room for Christian and Muslim as well as Hindu beliefs.

Thirty-five years ago, in Gandhi's heyday, an American missionary to India, home on furlough, said to me, "We missionaries know that someday India will be free. But our sympathies are with Great Britain. We know it is to our interest that British rule continue, for we know that as long as it does, we are free and we are protected. We don't know what will happen when India gets her freedom."

That missionary attitude of superiority and condescension—with its willingness to accept the patronage of the powers that be—is what the white Christians have had to unlearn. It does not go down any more. Gandhi's dream of "the unity of mankind under one God" leaves no place for favoritism.

The hallelujah faith lingers on in public worship, in hymns and formal prayers, and in the prayers at the inauguration of a president. It survives in the cathedral processionals of the American flag with the Christian flag behind the Cross and in the recitation of the historic creeds. But it fools nobody. Present-day Christians no more expect all the races of men to assemble under one name at Judgment Day than they look for the graves to be opened and the bodies to rise from the dead. Except for the hard core of fundamentalists, Christians no longer think they are sole heirs of salvation, keepers of the keys to the house of God and the gates of heaven. For better or for worse, they have joined the human race. Hallelujah!

It is almost impossible today to recall the imperious mood to which the missionary statesmen of Christendom rallied the faithful from 1910 to 1940, when missionaries were coming home in droves. The Red hammer and sickle was flying. The Christian hope of world dominion reached its high-water mark at about the time of the World Missionary Conference at Edinburgh, Scotland, in 1910. The meeting was called to parcel out the world for conquest. Leaders of the major Protestant denominations received reports from the mission fields, assessed the needs, and apportioned responsibility among the various churches represented. Rereading an account of the Edinburgh Conference proceedings in 1965, against the background of the two world wars and the anti-Christian revolutions in Europe, Asia, Africa, and the island empires, the story is incredible for childlikeness of faith, for romantic hopes, and self-congratulation.

The 1961 World Council of Churches assembly in New Delhi, India, was a flop for the news correspondents, the sponsoring denominations, even for the delegates; the wind was out of the sails. But in 1910 the hallelujah faith was magnificent. It had four years to go. The hallelujah faith was a happy faith while it lasted. It was not only sure of itself and of its ultimate universal triumph, but its home base was pleasant to contemplate. The Christian people, except the Negroes, were prosperous. The Catholics did not disturb the Protestants but kept to their parishes and their masses. Life was cleaner and more comfortable for the upper and middle classes that embraced most Protestants. Churchmen called conferences almost anywhere in the world at the drop of a hat; if the meeting was held in a colored country, the British navy could be depended upon to guarantee the safety of the visitors. The world was becoming a neighborhood in which war was unthinkable—as I heard in scores of sermons and addresses. William Jennings Bryan's most popular Chautauqua lecture was on "The Prince of Peace." The President of the United States in 1910 was a Unitarian, William Howard Taft, but his lineage was unimpeachable, and he believed in keeping the labor unions in their place. I heard a Methodist bishop praise Mr. Taft for his gracious manner toward trinitarian clergymen; he permitted the bishop to pray for him when he was ill. The main-line Protestant churches had their cornerstones laid by the Freemasons, so tolerant was the era.

The difference in mood and content of preaching between

the first two quarters of the present century was as wide and deep as the Grand Canyon—as wide as the ground between Søren Kierkegaard and Norman Vincent Peale.

The hallelujah faith of the first period was easy to sing, too— I remember our hearty singing at youth and mission rallies even better than the sermons; it was more fun, too. In 1912 Theodore Roosevelt's Progressive Party (to which many liberal preachers rallied) marched to defeat to a Christian hymn, and it seemed perfectly natural: "Onward, Christian Soldiers." That hymn out of a music-hall setting expressed the buoyant spirit of the times.

One of the rip-roaring hymns my generation sang when we were raising nickels and dimes for foreign missions:

> From all the dark places of earth's heathen races,
> O see how the thick shadows fly!
> The voice of salvation awakes every nation,
> "Come over and help us," they cry.

And the chorus went, "The Kingdom is coming." The stanzas were set to a jig tune, so the hymn wasn't used in churches where only good music was heard—a small minority indeed. I learned it by heart fifty years ago.

In those dear, dead days, John R. Mott was introduced to Christian and secular gatherings all over the world as "the foremost Christian statesman of our time." A founder and officer of the International Young Men's Christian Association, intimate of presidents, kings, and chancellors, Mott had what his admirers called "a world view of Christianity." This was a euphemism for Christian rule. When Mott spoke in the name of imperial Christendom, it was like listening to a British prime minister with an American accent.

I was thrilled to my toes by Mott throughout my youth and the exciting years of World War I. He brought my generation Rudyard Kipling supplemented by the Great Commission at the end of Matthew's Gospel: "Go ye therefore, and teach all nations." We had to take it as our manifest destiny. We knew nothing about other world religions, and cared less. Our public-school education had left us almost totally ignorant of the Far East. And all we knew about Darkest Africa was that the black man was better off in the American South.

Between 1910 and 1940 I interviewed scores of foreign missionaries home on furlough. They were as provincial as the folks at home. At their mission posts they lived in Western-style compounds where the natives never entered the front door but slippered around to the back door to do the hard labor for a handful of coins. Naked little girls were decently covered in pinafores and little boys with drawers. All were taught to sing "Jesus Loves Me"—in English, of course, since this was the foreordained language of salvation.

John R. Mott was the generalissimo of our crusade. A world traveler for more than fifty years (he lived to ninety), Mott was acquainted with every outpost of the Christian empire. When we sang "From Greenland's icy mountains, from India's coral strand" at church conventions and missionary conferences, we could see in our mind's eye brown and yellow and black heads bowing at the name of Christ like a field of wheat before the breeze, ripe for harvest. Compared to those festivals, the church conferences of the 1930s were pantywaist affairs; those youths who came after us had to settle for campfire talks on the "winsome Jesus."

Mott's career was as incredible as the period of history in which he was a dominant personage. Born the year of Appomattox, he had to wait till 1946 to share the Nobel peace prize "for his work in international church and missionary movements." His biographer, Basil Mathews, gives a list of the "leaders in Church and State" with whom Mott had interviews: Gandhi, Tolstoy, President Thomas G. Masaryk of Czechoslovakia, British Foreign Secretary Lord Edward Grey, Andrew Carnegie, Alexander Kerensky, "and most of the rulers of the nations of his time."

Mott was presiding chairman of the 1910 Edinburgh Conference, and, according to Matthews, this "made Mott a world

figure." His biographer says that in 1913 President Woodrow
Wilson was deeply disappointed when Mott refused appoint-
ment as ambassador to China. In 1917, Wilson sent Mott on a
special mission to Russia to study the physical and spiritual
needs of the war-devastated ally. Mott traveled a total of
1,700,000 miles in his lifetime, or sixty-eight times around the
world.

Mott's spectacular career—the last of its kind we are likely to
see—was a happy marriage of church and state such as the
Puritan theocrats of the "Holy Commonwealth" of New England never dreamed of. He was the last and the most eloquent
of our innocents abroad. He lived to see the China and India
and Russia he coveted for Christ go over the hill.

Mott had his victories, too, and they have outlived him. In
retirement homes today there are scores of men and women of
many denominations who were recruited by John R. Mott for
foreign missions. In dozens of countries over the world there
are community and national leaders whom he inspired and
encouraged and aided. And in some of those places there are
public and private educational and health institutions that
would never have come into existence without his help.

Mott was the inspiration and guiding hand of the Student
Volunteer Movement for Foreign Missions, an organization
that had tremendous influence on church college campuses.
He organized the World's Student Christian Federation and
served as general secretary and chairman. Everything he
touched had the whole world for its concern.

*The Evangelization of the World in This Generation* was the
title of a book by Mott published in 1900. It is filled with
quotations from Christian leaders around the world in support
of the book's ambitious program. Mott quotes a declaration of
Protestant missionaries to China in 1877: "We want China
emancipated from the thraldom of sin *in this generation*." (The
italics are in the original.)

Another memorable voice out of a happier past was that of
Sherwood Eddy. The preaching of this Boston liberal was com-

posed of equal parts Social Gospel and piety. He was a fearless crusader for social justice out of a background of wealth and privilege—not at all rare in Christian annals. Eddy understood what the American foreign missionary boards, including his own, learned too late: white Western Christianity must set its own house in order and let the plaster fall where it will. He was one of the first to plead for an end to the unholy alliances of the missionary with the trader and the colonial powers. For fifty years Sherwood Eddy was our noblest apostle of evangelism by reform and justice.

Like John R. Mott, Eddy was a world traveler, but his sympathies for the common man and the underprivileged brought him contacts with native leaders that Mott never enjoyed. Eddy knew China and India from the inside, not from insulated Western-style mission compounds. He was the national secretary of the Y.M.C.A. in India from 1896 to 1918, and thereafter for Asia. He knew Sun Yat-sen well. Blessed with incredible physical endurance and the most nearly perfect psychological balance of any man I have ever known, Eddy was unequaled for understanding, courage, and compassion. His appeals for repentance and reform beginning in our own house and the houses of our friends and allies, however, were conveniently forgotten.

Eddy had known Chiang Kai-shek throughout most of his career and was acquainted with many other leaders of the Kuomintang. In an interview, Eddy once told me the story of his personal appeals to Chiang for an end to the corruption and malfeasance in the Nationalist Chinese regime on the mainland. "I had lived too long in China, and traveled too much, not to perceive the creeping paralysis in Chiang's rule," Eddy said. "I warned him that while the Communists were wooing the peasants, his own power and prestige were slipping. The Chinese people still under Kuomintang rule were sick and tired of the war—they had known nothing but war and sacrifice and suffering since the death of Sun Yat-sen in 1925.

"Chiang was always cordial to me, although he knew I was

critical of his regime. He listened to me patiently, but I had the feeling I was talking to a deaf ear. His isolation from public opinion was almost complete. He gave me the impression he was the prisoner of the National Party—maybe he no longer had the power and influence I thought he had. He was looking for a miracle to save his dying cause." My managing editor cut this part of my interview with Eddy because it appeared to be critical of Washington's policy to sink or swim with Chiang.

Another picture of the last days of Chiang's army on the mainland, drawn for me by a returned American missionary, has something of a Sigmund Romberg operetta about it. This veteran missionary and his wife lived and served in Peking (Peiping) for more than forty years. Their children were born there and grew up speaking Chinese as early and as fluently as English. After the fall of Peking to the Communists in 1949, the missionary couple was held in house arrest for more than a year.

"We were prisoners, but were always well treated," the American repatriate told me. "Our old Chinese friends remained friends. When we were finally released, the Communists permitted my wife and me to ship our household goods home.

"The fall of Peking to the Red army happened on a weekend. One Thursday night we were amazed to see the lights come on in the city—we had lived under the blackout for eight years. I went to one of our Chinese neighbors for an explanation. He told me the Communists were just outside the city and had sent word they were moving in the next night. 'The Nationalist army must evacuate the city tonight,' my neighbor said, 'and the lights are on to prevent accidents while all those men and trucks and other equipment are moving out. Neither side wants any damage done to the city, and of course they don't want anybody to get hurt.'

"Sure enough, the next night all the lights were turned on again, and the Communist army came in, and nobody got hurt. But sometime Friday night," the missionary said, "we heard scattered rifle shots. The next morning I asked my Chinese neighbor about the shooting. He told me those were warning shots by the Communists. Some of the Nationalist troops were stragglers, hanging around the suburbs, so the shots were fired to warn them to get a hustle on." Thousands of hungry, ragged men from Chiang's armies deserted and threw away their arms, if they had any. Many surrendered to the Communists. Others tried to find their way home, often a long, heartbreaking journey.

If the many, many stories of our returned missionaries can be trusted to reflect the sentiments of the heart, American missionaries loved the Chinese people as no other people on earth. The Americans never saw their Chinese friends when they were prosperous, except for the comparatively small ruling class, who were too well placed to embrace a foreign faith. Yet how many times have I heard a returned missionary say of the Chinese, "They are the most wonderful people. They deserve everything and have so little."

Now the bamboo curtain has closed, and the world's greatest potential for a mission field has been lost—as far as that kind of influence can be lost. Monday-morning quarterbacking is easy: could the China story have been different? Perhaps only the missionaries know what was gained and what was lost.

I haven't heard a stirring sermon on foreign missions in ten years. Most of those I have heard since 1949 were lamentations over the failure of the Christian forces to strike while the iron was hot—before the atheistic Communists could recruit and train as many missionaries as the churches had. Instead of sermons on the evangelization of the world in a generation, there were stump speeches on Christianity versus communism.

High-school and college students and even theological seminarians are baffled and amused when an oldtimer tries to convey to them the hallelujah faith of the turn of the century. The world of that period is no more strange to them than its confident charm. They can hardly believe that even Christians and preachers and idealists could be so naïve.

The muting of the hallelujah faith in the face of the shrinkage
of Christian empire left preachers and churches as sharply
divided over public issues and alarms as they had always been
over the interpretation of Scripture, church government, and
holy orders. After the end of World War II, in the popular
preaching I heard, Christianity was presented as the only alter-
native to communism. Professional evangelists and Fundamentalist pastors lived by the godsent theme. They were swimming
with the tide of McCarthyism. Not only that, the fundamentalists had a new club to beat the heads of the modernists. Only
a baptized Christian who believed in the virgin birth could be
trusted to resist the wiles of communism. The Protestant fundamentalists were matched by the Roman Catholic Church,
which claimed it was the only dependable foe of atheistic communism; the claim became a burden to the pope with a million
Italian Communists in his front yard.

On a seventy-five-hundred-mile Western swing for my newspaper in 1944, I heard the fundamentalists attack modernism
and liberalism ad nauseam from local radio stations. The
preachers showed more talent for slander than knowledge of
either history or the mother tongue. The modernist clergy was
to blame for everything that kept the godfearing citizen awake
at night—from the apostasy of China and Eastern Europe to
the divorce rate, alcoholism, juvenile delinquency, and the
fluoridation of water.

At the same time I heard sermons on communism from pulpits in churches of all sizes and social standing. This was the
period of the national boom in religion, so congregations were
larger than I had ever seen.

The sermons I heard from liberal pulpits were not as cock-
sure as those by the fundamentalists—they never are. The mood
was chastened. There was no self-congratulation but instead a
searching examination of the sins of the West in general and
of the Christian people in particular. Those earnest preachers
asked how Marx and Lenin could collect a billion followers in
less time than it took American Protestantism to carry new

churches from the Tidewater to Kentucky. How could Holy
Russia, dotted with cathedrals and plastered with ikons and
swarming with priests and monks, fall to a rabble army in the
Bolshevik Revolution? Why did China fall to the Red army
when the country had been a favored field of Protestant missionary effort for a century and a half? Why were the intellectuals and artists and students alienated from the pulpit and
parish life? Why were the working classes everywhere indifferent toward the old established churches?

New nations were springing up by the dozen in the non-
European lands where the Christian missionary effort had been
concentrated. How many of them made any pretense of a Christian connection or choice?

After absorbing the shock of wars and revolutions and learning to pronounce the new strange names on the United Nations
roster, the old American missionary boards woke up to find
they were still in business at the old stands around the world,
the China mainland and a few smaller places excepted. The
Baptists were even still preaching in Moscow. What was new
in an old experience was the sign appearing with monotonous
regularity—Under New Management, which simply meant the
nationals. Native Christians and church members were beginning to practice what the foreign missionaries had been preaching to them all along—to stand on their own feet. They suddenly
realized that their many languages and dialects were transla-
table in heaven. The revolution in the old missionary Establishment—dark-skinned people coming out of the kitchens to take
over the front desks and the pulpits—was hard for the older
missionaries to take, much worse for their entrenched boards
and sponsors at home. For the newly enfranchised, the reversal
of roles was as exhilarating as a new flag or a new national
anthem. Sherwood Eddy would have led the cheering from the
top of Beacon Hill.

At the 1954 World Council of Churches assembly at Evanston, Illinois, there were three tall, dark, and handsome young
men in the crowded press room. They were journalists from

Indonesia, in the United States on grants for graduate study. Their English speech, dress, and manners were impeccable. One day, after we had become better acquainted, one of them said to a small group of American fellow correspondents, "Don't feel sorry for us. We are building a new nation. Didn't your American pioneers enjoy building this country?" And *that* is the new spirit in the old countries which we have quit calling heathen lands. They are still happy to have Western services—the manifold services in which the missionaries are expert—but they don't want us to feel sorry for them.

A beautiful example of an old type of service carried into the new day of missions is described in an article I wrote for the *United Church Herald* of August 22, 1963.

Halbert Earle (Bud) Hiteman and his wife Alice "used to operate a large-scale dairy farm near West Winfield, N.Y." Today they direct an Inter-Church Service team in a needy rural area in northwestern Greece; they teach and demonstrate just about everything that enriches human life on a farm, including the farmhouse and the village. A model farm, home canning, balanced diets, animal husbandry—"better goats, turkeys, rabbits and sheep." Better schools, recreation, even art. The Hitemans represent the Service Division of the United Church Board for World Ministries.

Their interchurch team "includes some two dozen young men and women from many countries and diverse Christian backgrounds"—a miniature United Nations making things hum on a model farm in Greece. This is a type of service in which Christian missionaries had grown gray before the Peace Corps was started.

The image and strategy of old missions in a new day—and new countries—are reflected in the person and services of a veteran missions worker and officer, Alford Carleton, executive vice president of the United Church Board for World Ministries, today's name for the oldest foreign missionary society in the United States, founded in 1810 as the American Board of Commissioners for Foreign Missions. Carleton's twenty-seven years of overseas service cover the period of the old foreign missionary attitudes and patronage and the beginnings of the revolution in Christian missions that still runs strong. He served in the Near East, a trouble spot, revolutionary area and point of conflict between East and West in the diplomacy of oil. From 1930 to 1954 Carleton served administrative posts in Turkey and Syria; before returning to the United States, he was president of Aleppo College in Syria. This put him in constant touch with the young leaders of the new nationalism and the rising masses.

A deeply committed Christian, this quiet-spoken man now deals from his New York office with the problems of Christian missions in a revolutionary world—with what he calls "the tremendous challenges of nation-building." Out of his rich background of experience in the Near East he is able to see the mission problems in terms of people, of faces and voices, hopes and dreams, conflicts and reconciliations. He is able to accept the changes and build on them. "The rise of nationalism colors every aspect of the Christian church's work on the continent of Africa," Carleton has said. "The churches with which the United Church of Christ works in Africa are all independent churches. Our missionaries work under their direction. The finest spirit of cooperation exists." I have heard the same declaration of the revised missionary thrust from other American missionaries to Africa—Methodist, Lutheran, Disciples, and Baptists.

"The day is past when Christian missions can be carried on from Western bases of support by consecrated men and women who live and think only as Americans," Carleton explains. "We must try to live and think as people in countries around the world."

He doesn't see himself and his co-workers as "taking" Christian missions anywhere, but rather as serving in the ranks of the cause wherever there is need and an open door. Who gets credit for what, and who takes precedence on the field, are old questions that have lost their point.

Carleton does have an old concern for missions that comes

out often in his talk and speeches and writing: how to stir the average American church member, "whose measure of caring for his climactic world is six cents a week" for missions.

I witnessed a moving and dramatic spectacle of the new day in missions—the revolution in the spiritual commerce between the old and new worlds—when I watched a group of twenty foreign students stand and look long and hard and silently at the old black church pew in the First Presbyterian Church in which Abraham Lincoln and his family sat when they were at home in Springfield, Illinois. The incident brought to mind what Alford Carleton had told me about "the tremendous challenges of nation-building."

It was the last Sunday in January 1965. The foreign visitors were all students from the University of Illinois at Urbana, an hour and a half's drive away. Forty-three of them made the trip in subzero weather to spend the weekend as guests of families of First Presbyterian Church and Westminster Presbyterian Church in the state capital.

The students came from eighteen countries in Africa, Asia, and Europe, and Cuba and Puerto Rico; about half of them from new nations. Their religions included Christianity, Islam, Hinduism, Shintoism, Judaism, and Buddhism. Some who professed no religious faith had attended Christian mission schools in their own homelands; then, out of their new knowledge, their new-won self-respect, and sharing the revolutionary spirit of their fellow countrymen, they framed their own declaration of independence. As a religious-news reporter after World War II, I met dozens of young foreign visitors at church and church-council conventions, most of them excited by the prospects for taking part back home in nation-building. These are the new clients of Christian world missions, and they will be treated as equals or they will be lost to the side of the West—no Lady Bountiful missions for them, no white man's burden.

The students, it seemed to me, showed more interest in the Abraham Lincoln pew than in the excellent sermon, the New Testament lessons, or the well-sung anthems of Brahms and

Christiansen. After they had marched past the pew, they joined the coffee hour in the church parlor where they exchanged their views of Lincoln—they had studied American history.

At the morning service I could see the students paying rapt attention to what the minister, Richard Paul Graebel, told them about Lincoln and his church pew: "Mrs. Lincoln belonged to the church, but Lincoln did not. In their time our pews were rented, and Lincoln paid his pew rent quarterly—we still have the canceled checks."

What were these students thinking about, I wondered, as they stood before the Lincoln pew? He was a nation-builder, too, a nation-saver in a time of civil war; and those mature students or their families have passed through civil wars. It was obvious from their behavior and talk that they were making a deep personal response to what they understood was the spirit of Lincoln—perhaps his magnanimity or his informal, unaligned faith. So he belonged to them too.

Alford Carleton, and a great company of Christian missionaries like him, rejoice to serve alongside the nation builders. They are friends, no longer strangers and foreigners. In their Christ there is no East nor West.

The hallelujah faith sank under the weight of the secular image it carried of Western culture and conquest. Its patronizing manner, its cultivated airs of superiority, were poison in the stream of life. The Christian mission for a revolutionary age has gone native. It carries no image except the Cross. Its claims are modest, its mood tentative. The modern missionary keeps his bags packed—he is one Christian who knows the meaning of the words, "For here ye have no continuing city. Sufficient unto the day is the evil thereof."

# 5

# Preaching, Politics, and Prohibition in the Roaring Twenties

During the national political campaign of 1920, Protestant churchgoers heard as much politics as gospel from their pulpits. There was not only the issue of the new League of Nations, which was already in deep trouble in a war-weary America. Woman suffrage (the Nineteenth Amendment) had been passed by Congress and was before the state legislatures for their certain approval.

Prohibition went into effect on January 16, 1920, under the Eighteenth Amendment and the strict Volstead Act. Within six months of passage—even before the national campaign got under way—the terrific problems of law enforcement were plain for all to see and deeply disturbing to public opinion, which was divided over the issue. The Presbyterian President Wilson was opposed to national prohibition; he had vetoed the Volstead Act, but Congress quickly passed it over his veto. Methodist bishops and preachers who had led the long fight for prohibition, taking the play away from the Anti-Saloon League, were determined to see a sincere effort made toward law enforcement.

The Democratic Party was suspect because its greatest voting strength lay no longer in the rural South but in the large population centers where prohibition was never popular, never obeyed. The Protestant clergy assumed that Republican Warren G. Harding would make a more dependable guardian of a dry country than his opponent, Governor James M. Cox. At a Methodist mass meeting in Illinois, Cox was denounced as "low, loose, and liquid"—an example of the scandalous depths to which the campaign had fallen in the churches.

It must be remembered, however, that prohibition never had the backing of half the Protestant churches and clergy. Its religious backers were a powerful minority, a well-organized Washington lobby.

An unfortunate by-product of the prohibition era and the 1920 campaign was a heating up of old animosities between Protestant and Catholic Americans. This development reached its first but not its last peak in the campaign of 1928 when Governor Alfred E. Smith became the first Roman Catholic candidate of a major party for the Presidency. That year was the lowest point in American politics since Abraham Lincoln's first campaign. In Kentucky alone, six deaths were attributed to election-day fracases.

When Candidate Smith's special train reached Jefferson City, the state capital of Missouri, early one Sunday morning, the train was stopped in the yards in order that Smith and his wife might attend mass. Not long after, I was present when a Baptist minister told a small group of pastors, "You know that when Smith left his train at Jefferson City he was so dog drunk he had to be helped from his Pullman to an automobile, then half carried to his pew in the cathedral." I heard the same story, with variations, a dozen times; the last time at a church dinner where the talebearer was the wife of a prominent industrialist. She made the story worse by adding a vicious remark about Mrs. Smith's looks—"Can you imagine *that* woman in the White House?"

Prohibition and the League of Nations were temporary crises in church life. But there was another problem that refused to be settled. This was the running feud between religious beliefs and the findings and theories of science. This historic contro-

versy goes to the heart of faith and the authority of revealed
religion, as the religionists well understand. In a country with
public-school education, its ramifications reach everybody.

In sixty years I have heard more sermons on the subject of
Science versus Religion than on any other theme. The debate,
however, has generated more heat than light.

In the modern world that science made, the ordeal of faith
overlaid the happy years of Protestant domination between
1880 and 1930. Robert G. Ingersoll's *Some Mistakes of Moses*
was published in 1879 and was still selling well at the turn of
the century. The famous agnostic author died in 1899. As a
churchgoing farm boy I heard Ingersoll's lectures and publications cursed and discussed along with the weather and crop
reports. I took part in further discussions during recess periods
at our one-room district school, out of hearing of our prim and
proper schoolteachers. At Sunday school, my class of boys was
warned by our woman teacher to avoid Ingersoll's evil influence
as we were expected to shun evil companions, cigarettes, and
profanity. Our redheaded village blacksmith kept a copy of
*Some Mistakes* at his shop to bait the pious farmers who brought
their horses to be shod and plowshares to be sharpened. I was
twelve years old when I discovered a copy in my brother-in-
law's library and tried to read it when nobody was looking. In
the newspaper rooms of my maturity, Ingersoll was old hat to
men and women who could not imagine that modern scientists
might be mistaken. My grandchildren now in college have
never heard of Bob Ingersoll. They never dispute science either.

When I enrolled in McKendree College in 1913, the only
member of the faculty who didn't, in private, accept the general
teaching of evolution was the president, a self-educated minister and evangelist. His three-hour course in the Bible, which
was required, consisted almost entirely of a literal interpretation of Scripture. But since our teacher was away most of the
time raising money for the school, the course was not arduous.
Besides, everybody got a passing grade.

Ten years later, evolution was a hot potato in church-related colleges all over the country; many teachers and preachers, too, lost their jobs.

Ironically, the most quoted Protestant spokesman in the melee over Genesis versus Darwin was neither an ordained minister nor a reputable theologian but a layman and politician, William Jennings Bryan, who died five days after the close of the Scopes "monkey" trial in Dayton, Tennessee. The star performers in that *opéra bouffe* were Bryan for the state, and Clarence Darrow for the defense; their words and posturings were praised and damned in hundreds of pulpits for months on end. The courtroom battle was a draw, but faith took an awful beating outside.

The one time I heard Bryan defend Genesis and attack Darwin was in a church-sponsored lecture. He poked fun at what he said was a teaching of science, that the human eye was the development by slow evolution of a skin protuberance which resembled a wart. Bryan's crushing rejoinder was, "I'm sure glad one of those warts didn't grow on top of my head."

In 1920, the Methodist Church, flush with its victory for prohibition, held a world rally on the Ohio State Fairgrounds at Columbus. There were dozens of missionary exhibits and special programs. The fairgrounds swarmed with Christian nationals—individuals and families—of all races, continents, and from many lands. There were bishops by the score. The theme of the Methodist meeting was "Christ or Chaos." The slogan became a popular sermon topic for several years.

The most popular feature attraction of the Methodist fair was a trombone choir of one hundred pieces. Many of the trombones were made especially for the occasion in order to complete the voicing and harmony of such a large instrumental group limited to only one instrument. So successful was the musical experiment that listeners were able to sit on the grass within ten feet of the massed trombone choir or a hundred yards away with equal delight.

The most famous platform guest at the fair was Bryan. He

stood on a small chair in order to be seen and heard by the more than ten thousand people in the open air. His long address, I remember, made poor copy for the news because it was stale—a hodgepodge of his political liberalism and religious fundamentalism. But Bryan was the darling of the Methodists for his assistance in putting over prohibition.

The 1920 Methodist meeting was significant for an incident that went unpublicized. The climax of the ten-day affair was a pageant with hundreds of costumed performers portraying, in biblical speech, the slow but steady march of mankind from darkness to light under the banner of Christ the King. Of course, the music for the pageant included selections from Handel's *The Messiah*, with opera stars in leading roles, supported by a chorus of a thousand voices assembled from church choirs. The costly colored program of the pageant included, as a part of this march, a long episode on the League of Nations as the latest embodiment of man's unquenchable longing for peace. This episode was omitted in the performance. In 1920 the issue of United States membership in the League of Nations was a political issue in the national campaign. The Democratic Party supported membership; the Republican Party was skeptical to the point of practical opposition. The sponsors of the Methodist pageant yielded their faith and hope to political pressure. But none of them would discuss the ticklish problem with the reporters. In those days the Methodists, like big business, were never really happy under a Democratic administration.

The Ku Klux Klan had reappeared in 1915, and during the 1920s it rose quickly to fantastic power in both the South and the North, and enrolled thousands of church members and many ministers. I knew several ministers, in southern Illinois, Indiana, and Massachusetts, who acted as recruiting agents for the Klan for a generous commission. The terror lasted about ten years, and then seemed to disappear.

The Klan was not only anti-Catholic, anti-Semitic, anti-Negro, and fiercely nativistic; it was also extremely fundamentalist in its religious approach—and its leaders played the religious angle for all it was worth. In hundreds of communities large and small the Klan was the archenemy of the liberal clergy. Klansmen in their flowing white sheets, hooded and wearing masks, marched silently into churches in the middle of the worship service, deposited money on the collection plate, and left without speaking a word. It was not a gesture of religious devotion, and every grown person in the house knew this. It was both a salutation and a dramatic warning. The church and its minister were put on notice that they were being watched by the secret order which represented power and was not afraid to act.

Ministers told me they were troubled and afraid because they had no way of knowing how many Klansmen were members of their congregation. One southern Illinois pastor said that out of three hundred men in his church, he was certain that at least two hundred were Klansmen; he walked the tightrope in the pulpit after being warned that the Klan was in a position to wreck his church finances and send him on his way.

One day in August 1927, I visited Herrin, Illinois, a few miles from my birthplace, and inspected the chipped brick in the walls of the largest hotel on Main Street, made on April 13, 1926, in bloody battle. Gang warfare had broken out in Herrin and surrounding "bloody" Williamson County when bootlegging and rumrunning became profitable. Local police did nothing to enforce the prohibition law, so flamboyant Glenn Young was engaged by a group of citizens, including clergy, to lead Ku Klux Klan forces against the bootleggers. He and his armed Klansmen made more than four hundred raids, including some on private houses. The county sheriff represented the opposition to the Klan. Some of his deputies were former bootleggers; Ora Thomas was one of them. Glenn Young was shot down at the hotel cigar counter by Ora Thomas; two minutes later, Thomas was riddled by Klan gunfire. A pitched battle followed in the streets.

I visited the cemetery at the edge of Herrin and saw the two

rows of graves facing each other across the gravel driveway—
casualties of the gun battles in town and in the county. At the
head of one row of graves was the mausoleum of Klansman
Young, and exactly opposite, the ornate tomb of Ora Thomas—
the rivals were still leading their armed gangs, and the unlucky
mobsters in humble graves faced one another in death as they
had in life.

In the five-year period up to the pitched battle of April 13,
1926, forty-one men met violent deaths in the Herrin area;
eleven more were killed later. The Klan claimed twenty-five
hundred members in Williamson County, out of a population
of some forty thousand. Churches and ministers were under
terrific pressure from the Klan to take sides, while the citizens
went in fear of their lives.

In the summer of 1924 I was taken to a regional rally and
massive initiation ceremony of the Ku Klux Klan in open fields
near Worcester, Massachusetts. When I was invited by the
presiding Kleagle to pronounce the invocation to open the
meeting, he asked me, "Have you ever prayed in front of thirty
thousand men before?"

The speaker's platform was the bed of a two-ton truck, and
from where I stood, the crowd of men in front of me, stretching
far across the pasture land, looked like a million. The scanty
newspaper reports and radio the next day estimated the crowd
at from twenty to thirty thousand.

When the chairman introduced me, he told the crowd, "We
always have the clergy with us, for they know we are right."
He was the sales manager of a wholesale firm in Connecticut
and, I was told, in charge of Klan recruiting and initiation for
New England. The mass meeting that night was the culmina-
tion of an intensive and widespread drive for members.

I had, of course, no advance notice that I would be called on
to give the invocation. The spectacle of thousands of men
gathered in semidarkness in a secret and heavily guarded
meeting on what New Englanders call a mowing (meadow-
land) was almost overwhelming. Fortunately for my compo-

sure, I remembered a short prayer I had used at a recent memorial Sunday service in my church; I repeated it slowly, giving it all the diaphragm propulsion I had:

"O Lord, father of mankind and governor of nations, we bring to thee for thy favor our beloved land. Thou hast blessed us beyond measure: in thy great mercy continue thy favor in order that we may be known as thy people dwelling under thy care—and under thy judgment. May the citizens delight to do thy will—make them to know thy will. Thou didst lead our forefathers in establishing this nation in liberty and justice— may we never fail to cherish the blessings of liberty and justice.

"Guide the president of the United States and all others in authority: give them wisdom, a good understanding, courage, and a sincere love of righteousness and mercy and truth.

"We thank thee, O Lord, for the blessings of peace: keep us in peace, and may all the nations of the earth dwell together in peace and brotherhood.

"Bless the homes and families of our land: keep them in safety, in harmony and love, free from strife, rejoicing not in iniquity, but rejoicing in the truth. So may we hold fast the liberty in which we stand, and remain in thy favor; for thine, O Lord, is the power and the majesty and the glory for ever. Amen."

At that time, I was pastor of the Congregational Church in Grafton, Massachusetts, eight miles from Worcester. I was dumfounded when I was invited by a member of my congregation to go with him to the Klan conclave. Will Greene was a member of an old New England family, a successful salesman and the owner of considerable property including a beautiful colonial house. I had regarded Greene, one of my closest friends in town, as a genuine liberal.

When he picked me up at the parsonage, he already had three men in his car, all Klansmen. We drove to the courthouse in Worcester and stopped across the street. A man stepped from the curb and gave Greene his directions. When we reached the outskirts of Worcester, I noticed the first long white paper

arrow posted on a tree beside the road. We followed the white
arrows to the secret meeting place, making many turns, picking
up other cars along the way, all loaded with men. By the time
we reached the last paved road and were in sight of the meeting
place, we were in a procession of hundreds of automobiles.
Many of the men carried their Klan sheets and hoods, but none
put them on until they had left their cars.

We turned into a dirt lane that led about three hundred yards
to the meeting place. Several Klansmen in their sheets and
hoods, but with their faces showing, stood guard at the open
gate to the lane and checked every car. Each driver vouched
for his passengers after whispering a password into the guard's
ear. This checkpoint was a roadblock, and the meeting was
delayed over an hour because of the traffic jam at the gateway.

The cars were parked in a giant U around the arena facing
the inside, and their lights were left on until the initiation
started. There was also moonlight until near the end of the
meeting.

The speaker's truck platform was lighted by gasoline torches,
and other torches lighted the open space between the truck and
the standing crowd. Small tables were in place in the open
space, with two clerks at each table; they were collecting the
ten-dollar membership fees, and there were lines of men before
each table. This business continued right up to the initiation.
The silence of the great crowd was eerie—like an army of the
deaf and dumb.

Of course, I was wondering where all those men came from
and what they thought they were doing here. The chairman
told me there were more than two hundred ministers in the
crowd. I recognized a Baptist pastor from North Grafton,
Massachusetts, who had boasted to me that he made more
money recruiting members for the Klan, at a fee of five dollars,
than he made from preaching. He urged me to join his racket.

I learned from my host of the evening that many of those
thousands of men came from small towns, villages, and farms
all over central Massachusetts. And most of those who came

from Worcester and other cities had migrated to those population centers from small towns and farms. I was welcomed by
a grocer's deliveryman from North Grafton whom I knew; he
shook my hand but didn't speak a word. The men I saw that
night were not the prosperous class; they were still in their
work clothes or in cheap slacks and shirts. There were too
many old cars on the field. These were little guys at home, the
unorganized labor of outstate Massachusetts; they were drilled
to work under bosses, and they were afraid of losing their jobs
to "shanty Irish" or other immigrants, or they were out on the
night's adventure from rocky farms which other men owned.
This meeting of the Klan was the only place where their birth-
right citizenship was recognized—the officeholders in town
never remembered their names till a week before election. On
this field of militant virtue, "aroused citizenship," they stood
shoulder to shoulder with other Knights of the Invisible Empire.
They carried secrets which the "fish-eaters" could only guess
at—and fear. Many of them had tears in their eyes when the
initiation ceremony was over and the meeting broke up.

As an outsider I was permitted, after my prayer, to stand on
the ground by the speaker's truck until it was time for the initiation ceremony. The Kleagle spoke for half an hour. He began
with a fervent tribute to the clergy, dwelling on the hardships
and sacrifices of the ministers of small churches. "These men
of God are the most important men in the country, and we are
starving them to death. You men ought to be ashamed of your-
selves—how much do you pay your preacher? I tell you, get
behind these men of God. Hold up their hands. Let them know
where you stand"—a double-edged remark if I ever heard one.

From time to time the speaker grasped the folds of the large
American flag flown from a standard fastened to the truck at
his right hand, and added a stirring call for more patriotism.
Most of his speech was a sales talk, and here he hit his stride.
It was a rabble-rousing appeal to the men to bring in more
members—he took time to praise the men who at the moment
were paying their fees at the tables. He said that national

membership in the Klan had reached five million, but he wouldn't be satisfied till it had doubled that mark, "and then some." He said that the Klan must have a greater membership than any political party—"Then we'll show those weak-kneed politicians who's running the show. When we are through, they'll know who this country belongs to."

The Kleagle closed his speech with a few remarks that surprised me: "We are guardians of the courts and of justice. We are keeping watch over local courts and magistrates to see that justice is done, no funny business. We aim to see that the rich and poor are treated alike." This brought a tremendous roar of shouted applause from the crowd.

Now it was time for the secret initiation ceremony. The moment the speaker ended, I was seized by one of the dozen or so armed guards surrounding the truck, a young man in an old army uniform. He hustled me, with unnecessary roughness, to the far side of another and smaller truck parked about fifty yards behind the speaker's stand. There I found I had company in detention—a young man who was crying but not in fear; he was foreign-born and his application for Klan membership had been rejected. He was a German immigrant, a grease monkey in a Worcester garage. He was a renegade Catholic who had turned against his church. He was the charge of a second young armed guard. The guards quickly passed an inch rope around our waists and tied us together, and each guard held his end of the rope.

The initiation ceremony had started—my watch showed eleven-thirty. The only light was from the torches in the open space in front of the crowd. My fellow prisoner and I could hear voices speaking, a couple of times snatches of singing, but we could not make out the words, and of course we could not see anything.

The initiation took another hour. I was released and permitted to walk back to the speakers' truck; the German immigrant stayed behind.

Before the burning of the cross—the climax of the night, and

a sort of benediction—the Kleagle made a strange announce-
ment: "We have word from our scouts that Senator Walsh's big
black limousine has been seen cruising in the neighborhood."
(David Ignatius Walsh, a Roman Catholic, was United States
Senator from Massachusetts from 1919 till his death in 1947.)
"The Senator isn't in his car but he filled it with his henchmen.
I must warn you that our enemies are always lying in wait.
Drive carefully, keep a sharp lookout for ambush, and stay close
together as long as you can."

At the arena, all lights were turned off and the vast assem-
blage of men was in complete darkness and silence when a
huge cross, fifteen feet tall, standing on top of a low hill behind
the crowded field, was lighted; the Klansmen turned around to
face it, their hats off. The cross burned spectacularly for several
minutes—it was reported to have been seen ten miles. A flaming
cross lighting up the darkness of midnight on a field of hate.

The next day's newspapers reported that several fights broke
out on the Klansmen's way home, rocks were thrown at their
cars, one Klansman was shot to death. There was another report
that three men were killed, but this was not verified.

# 6

# From Billy Sunday
# to Billy Graham

Who that heard it could ever forget Billy Sunday's most famous
sermon—on the evils of intoxicating beverages? When I heard
it, the long fight for national prohibition was nearing the climax
of victory for the drys, and the famous ballplayer-turned-
evangelist gave his sermon muscle. Woodrow Wilson had been
elected to his second term as President, but Sunday had little
respect and no affection for his fellow Presbyterian in the White
House. Teddy Roosevelt's "strenuous life" posture was much
more to his gymnastic taste, and Sunday took many jibes at
"that Princeton professor." Babe Ruth was mowing the batters
down as the best left-handed pitcher the Boston Red Sox had
brought up in a coon's age—Billy Sunday took more sermon
illustrations from the baseball diamond than from the Bible;
his knowledge of the Bible was limited. His sermon on liquor
was superb showmanship right out of the George M. Cohan
era, complete with the flag.

Picture a barnlike coliseum seating ten thousand persons
where Caruso had sung; a big bare platform with a reading
desk on which the preacher laid his Bible and manuscript—yes,
Billy Sunday had a manuscript, though with his athletic
prowess he could leap ten feet from it and back again without
losing his place. He always gave this sermon on a Sunday after-

noon, and today his crowd started gathering three hours before it was time for the service to begin; most of them came by streetcar or on foot. It was a merry throng, like people on holiday.

Homer Rodeheaver and his trombone were a national image —Billy Sunday's song leader, his confidant and his handy memory, end man for the preacher's vaudeville. Rody, as Sunday called him, was utterly charming, one of the most ingratiating personalities in the religious world of a time that was long on sobriety and short on humor. Rody's first job was to warm up the crowd—he could get a vast audience of untrained voices to sing the old gospel songs like a muny opera chorus. But his crowd was always impatient for his trombone solo.

The preacher and the song leader engage in conversational asides at various points in the long, chatty prayer—somewhat like an over-the-back-fence talk between congenial neighbors. "O Lord, you remember that baldheaded banker in Syracuse?— Rody, that was Syracuse, wasn't it?" "No, Billy, it was Baltimore." "O Lord, remember that baldheaded banker in Baltimore—he raised money for you and got blood out of a turnip." Ten thousand people watching and listening, afraid of missing the punch line of the show that they might enjoy most, laughing, nudging one another, shouting, applauding.

A stagehand carries in a huge glass jar and sets it at front center on the platform; it looks like a demijohn with the wickerwork removed. Billy Sunday sticks a small American flag in the jar, then jerks it out, and grimaces. Puts a small bunch of flowers in the jar, jerks them out. Holds his nose. Ties a bow of pretty ribbon around the neck of the jar, rips it off. Then he calls for an axe (not a hammer, as I have seen reported), strips off his coat, rolls up his shirtsleeves, waits till the noisy crowd has subsided into dead silence, and smashes the glass jar (the hated liquor traffic) into smithereens with one mighty blow. An ovation from the people. Half of the men in the congregation will have beer when they get home.

Forty years pass. Billy Sunday has been in his grave twenty

years. A new generation of Protestants has never heard a barn-storming evangelist. Two world wars have buried their dead. The Korean War has brought a new burst of prosperity and the car-hungry people are trying to forget Pearl Harbor and Bataan. The St. Louis Arena, a sports palace large enough to handle horse shows and the Icecapades, is filled with fourteen thousand people on a Sunday night in winter when the temperature outside is only a few degrees above zero, snow and ice on the streets and parking lots, an arctic wind blowing, driving hazardous, and most public meetings in the city are canceled by the bad weather. I am sitting in the press box on the floor at one side of the high, square platform on which the microphones gleam. Billy Graham pulls up a collapsible chair beside mine and sits down to talk about the weather. He is the coolest, calmest person in the house. Nobody who didn't know the young man would guess that he is tonight's attraction. He is a handsome man, well over six feet, in his very-blue blue suit. "I hope nobody gets hurt tonight," he says. "I'm always worried about traffic accidents." Then he asks me for news of other religion editors whom he hasn't seen since his last crusade —he calls a dozen of them by their first names. He carries his Bible and sermon manuscript in his left hand.

On the platform, George Beverly Shea, Billy Graham's song leader, is breaking the ice and thawing out the crowd with solos and community singing. Shea, who looks like a Hollywood glamour boy, is a humble man—like Homer Rodeheaver—and the news-media corps holds him in affection. His recordings are best sellers. By the magic of his stylish appearance and voice and wit, Shea transforms the cavernous hall into a warm and friendly meeting place; the service becomes an hour and a half of reverent worship. The evangelist does not appear on the platform until it is time for his sermon. This is showmanship not out of the bush leagues but from Madison Avenue—every act of the performance is clicked off with professional precision. The Billy Graham staff, with the voluntary aid of a large local committee of clergy and laymen, has planned and advertised the meeting for weeks in advance; even the ushers are trained by rehearsal.

Graham reads his sermon tonight rather carefully and, to one who has heard him many times, more slowly than his custom was. He begins, "This sermon was not easy to write. It is not going to be easy to preach—I had rather not preach this sermon." His subject is the inescapable judgment of a righteous God on sinners and a sinful world. I had heard the same theme in sermons time without number, beginning with brush arbor meetings fifty years ago. But what a difference! Graham's voice has a magnetism that is not lost on television and radio. The organ tones seem to come from far back in his throat. His articulation is superb. His voice rises to emphasis, increasing in volume without the least trace of physical exertion. And it is free from the curse of the unctuous pulpit tone—Holy Willie's margarine quality.

After the sermon, Graham makes his altar call. Shea again takes over on the platform and leads the congregation in singing familiar gospel songs—hymns of invitation. Several hundred persons make their way from seats in every corner of the arena to the foot of the platform to give public witness of their "decision for Christ"—in the words of the evangelist, "to take Jesus Christ as their personal savior." Most of the converts are youths and young men and women.

I have heard Billy Graham in many places, when he preached or talked informally to small groups, to assemblies of ministers, and to a congregation of twenty-five thousand persons. I have heard him in churches and tabernacles and municipal auditoriums and public parks, at luncheon clubs and press conferences, on radio and television. I have sat or stood ten feet away as he preached to great crowds that were friendly and responsive, and on other occasions when he faced smaller gatherings that were critically skeptical, politely hostile—liberal clergy, college students, and news-media personnel. When Graham is in top form and sound physical condition he could charm a snake out of its skin.

I heard Billy Graham deliver a long sermon to fifteen thousand persons in Miami Beach, where he drew larger crowds than the most spectacular sports events. Every public speaker knows there is no more severe test of his skill and powers than to establish rapport with a vast audience in an arena-type auditorium with temporary seating fanned out over a half acre. Billy Graham accomplished this feat in Miami Beach almost instantly and apparently without studied effort. In fact, I had a conversation with him five minutes before he went to the platform, and he was relaxed, almost gay in mood. And with the first ringing sounds of his voice the crowd was in his hand.

Graham has always insisted on integrated meetings for his crusades. His hardest fight for his principle of integration was in Memphis, Tennessee, years ago. The chairman of the local committee sponsoring the crusade and the largest financial backer withdrew his support when Graham refused to yield on the point of integration. A second auditorium was found, after the first choice was closed to him, and Graham went on to hold a successful series of meetings.

I had a long talk with Graham in his hotel room on a day when he was to speak at a luncheon of a large association of Negro ministers. He was ill and taking medicine for a throat affliction that has troubled him off and on for many years. "The Lord didn't endow me with a strong constitution," he said. "I don't expect to live to be an old man, so I must work while it is yet day." We talked about his engagement to address the Negro pastors. "I didn't know much about the race problem when I started preaching," Graham said. "In fact, I didn't know too much about anything. I had to learn the hard way as I went along."

When Graham arrived at his meeting with the Negro ministers, the atmosphere in the dining hall was about as cordial as a public hanging. But he talked to them as frankly as he had talked to me in his hotel room, telling about the same story of his experience in learning the facts of life. Then he answered questions for half an hour. His hostile audience was won over; he was held for another half hour so the Negro pastors could introduce themselves to him and shake his hand. And they joined his crusade.

In 1960 I attended a press conference where Graham was pressed by a couple of hostile reporters to state his choice for president, Protestant Richard M. Nixon or Catholic John F. Kennedy. No secretary of state could have displayed neater footwork than the evangelist in getting out of that corner. He kept his politics a mystery wrapped in smiles and a general concern for the welfare of the nation.

Big city newspapers, many of them being anticlerical and antiprohibition, had a field day with Billy Sunday's borderline vulgarity. ("I was invited to a high society banquet one night, and when I got home my wife asked me what the ladies wore. I told her I was too much of a gentleman to look under the table.") How many times was I embarrassed by the ribald remarks of newspaper associates about the published accounts of the evangelist's meetings!

Billy Graham is also a master of the vernacular, but he is strait-laced in speech and vocabulary. In the pulpit or out of it, he is always the Southern Baptist gentleman on his best plantation behavior. He is an old-fashioned Carolinian. His pulpit and private manner, his voice and general bearing, as well as the professional organization and promotion of his crusades, are extremely sophisticated. Religion editors have remarked that Graham has enjoyed the biggest, slickest build-up of any clergyman in the history of American Protestantism.

The truth about Billy Sunday's spectacular success (popularity) in the first quarter of the century has never been told. I have read several books about him, and all were unsatisfactory to one who was there. Sunday's pulpit gymnastics and his jokes, his baseball lingo, his colorful, often inspired epithets for hypocrites and stuffed shirts, and his "corn" were never accepted by the majority of churchgoing Protestants. Such carryings-on were unbecoming, or "common," as my generation would have said. And Billy Sunday didn't give a ballplayer's damn whether the churches supported him or not—he played all the positions on his team.

Sunday was a natural, one of the boys. He didn't need a

public-relations bureau like Billy Graham's to tell him where a freewheeling evangelist's chips were. They were not in spats. The old established churches with their patrician ministers were the fall guys for his minstrel-show wisecracks—his mimicry of an overstuffed parson in a plush pulpit was sure-fire. His popularity as a one-man show was in inverse ratio to the esteem in which religious faith was held and to the moral and spiritual authority of the churches with the masses of men, and no one understood this better than he. He drew great crowds because he vulgarized his Bible texts and comments to flatter the vulgar mind, which enjoys nothing more than take-offs on people who take themselves seriously, and to make light of a serious tradition—anti-intellectualism was a national sport in Sunday's time. So his piety-draped vaudeville won a popular following everywhere because it fitted public taste like hamburgers with onions.

Billy Sunday's rough-and-tumble preaching fifty years ago drew men and women, more men than women, whom church members called sinners; and Sunday encouraged them to believe they were probably as good and as pious as the deacon in spats away from home at an Elks convention. Not many sinners go to hear Billy Graham. Sunday's crowds were a cross section of the population—bums to millionaires. Graham's larger crowds are made up largely of church members: Southern Baptists like the evangelist, and men and women from the fundamentalist revivalistic sects. They come to hear the old gospel from a new and famous voice—what they had listened to in small churches and tabernacles they are now hearing from the housetops. The majority of his following represent whole congregations of fundamentalist Christians; dozens of busloads of them had reserved train coaches, some of them coming from a distance of a hundred and fifty miles.

Billy Sunday played to the galleries like an old trouper. At the peak of the prohibition crusade, his sermon on the evils of drinking was as dramatic as *Ten Nights in a Barroom*. When World War I came, he turned fire-eater; his scorn for the pacifist was in the best form of the recruiting sergeant. He was extremely conservative in his social views and never failed to court the approval and support of the powers that be in business, finance, and politics. He made all manner of fun of the Social Gospel, which was going strong in his day.

Billy Sunday also had his victories. For all his antics, his playing to the grandstand, he accomplished good. This I know firsthand. Many, many men who had not been to church since they were married went to hear the famous preacher out of curiosity, were shamed by his pinpointed unclerical descriptions of their sins and follies, hit the sawdust trail to the altar, and went away newborn men. They quit drinking and gambling and swearing and forsook old evil companions, and went home to their families and thereafter led upright lives. I have known stalwart churchmen, elders and deacons and trustees, Sunday-school teachers and prayer leaders, who were converted and reformed under Sunday's preaching. By his unorthodox, flamboyant methods he was able to do on a wholesale scale what the Salvation Army had been doing one by one—what the old established churches were never willing to undertake.

Compared to Billy Sunday's barnstorming, Billy Graham's methods depend upon organization, publicity, and follow-up with his converts that function like an I.B.M. machine; nothing is left to chance or inspiration.

Followers and critics of Graham—religion editors too—agree that the primary appeal of his preaching is its extreme simplicity: believe the Bible. There is really only one problem in the world: Sin. Sin arises in the personal life and infects public life. Graham lumps together all the problems of the lonely, lost individual soul and the whole rolling stellar universe and gives a solution that a normal child can understand: "Take Jesus Christ as your personal Saviour." All the rest will follow: personal welfare and happiness, industrial and international peace, brotherhood and justice. This summary of Graham's preaching is also the definition of fundamentalism. In this respect Sunday and Graham are ideological twins.

The private enterprise nature of Billy Graham's preaching

also tells us why he is the darling of Protestant industrial tycoons and Protestant politicians. No preacher since Billy Sunday, not even Norman Vincent Peale, has enjoyed the confidence of corporation executives and presidents of the United States and members of Congress as Graham has. He is especially appreciated by elected officials whose lives would be so much easier if only everybody lived by the Golden Rule. Graham is equally at ease on the country club golf course and Jack Parr's television show.

Where Billy Sunday relied on muscle and invective and hyperbole to cut and slash his way, Billy Graham's crusading is gentle and dignified and restrained—a combination of the methods of a salesman, lawyer, teacher and personal counselor. The charm of his personality—his spirit and style—that wins attention and confidence face to face and across the vast expanse of a great auditorium or open air stadium is due in part to the fact that he has never lost his boyish nature—at forty-seven, Graham is still disarmingly a boy at heart. The big crowds and public acclaim—and White House visits—have left his natural disposition unspoiled. Graham is a fundamentalist in ideas and a professional in performance, but he is never pompous.

In 1918 I sat in on a meeting of a dozen liberal ministers who were holding a post-mortem on a Billy Sunday revival in their city that had drawn large crowds for four weeks. These ministers had taken no part in the evangelistic campaign beyond attendance at several meetings. They were, of course, critical of Sunday's fundamentalist views of scripture, but they were far more critical of his prankish pulpit style. "His big meetings are a circus for the multitude, a great big hullabaloo." "He shows contempt for the dignified pulpit, and no understanding whatever of what the regular pastor tries to do in his church." "Billy Sunday is a passing show; he will be forgotten when he is no longer able to keep up his gymnastics." "He depends upon excitement and entertainment and the sawdust trail to get results, so his so-called converts will melt away when the enthusiasm of Billy Sunday's presence has gone." Those pastors reported that they, all of them together, had received fewer than a dozen new church members from the month's revival.

In 1952 I heard another small group of liberal ministers conduct a post-mortem on a Billy Graham crusade of twenty-eight nights in their city. They had heard the young evangelist a few times but had not supported his campaign; neither had their churches. They had received many signed cards from the local crusade committee signifying a desire to join certain churches, but none of the signers had appeared in person. Two of the ministers said they expected "in time" to receive a few new members from their prospect cards.

These ministers, like their liberal brethren of 1918 with Billy Sunday, dismissed Graham's view that the Bible is wholly inspired and without error. They were skeptical of mass evangelism as a means of recruiting church members. But their sharpest criticism was leveled at Graham's altar call for "decisions for Christ." One man called it "a gimmick" unworthy of Christian evangelism. The pastor of an old church and a national officer of his liberal denomination said, "This business of 'decisions for Christ' gives me the impression of arrogance, though I'm sure Billy Graham doesn't mean to give that impression. Here is a man who presumes to offer eternal salvation to anyone who agrees with him and answers his call to the altar. What right does Billy Graham have—and where does he get the authority —to divide the sheep from the goats as men and women walk down the aisle and gather on the floor in front of the platform? Is he competent to read the eternal destinies of human beings whom he has never seen before? Does he know the secret and the mysteries that the rest of us must take on faith?"

# 7

# Big Names
# and Bad Times

Harry Emerson Fosdick was seventy-five years old when he
went to St. Louis to deliver the annual Reformation Day sermon.
It was a bad time in the nation's history: morale was low and
church attendance was high; religious fervor was at an all-time
high. The long, painful, humiliating negotiations for peace in
Korea had begun at Panmunjon that week. What was called
a "police action" in Korea had left American public opinion
deeply and bitterly divided—the country had endured no such
humiliation (settling for a truce) since the British burned the
Capitol and the White House in 1814. Potomac piety was as
popular as the new President, General Dwight D. Eisenhower.

The St. Louis municipal auditorium was filled long before the
October night service began with more than ten thousand persons. Several thousand more were turned away. The preacher's
subject was the reformation that is never finished in church
and lay life—a stirring call for a rededication to Christian ideals
and hopes, and one more crusade to bring peace and justice
to a stricken world.

Fosdick's great congregation listened closely to every word
—the glorious voice had lost none of its power. It was one of
the best Fosdick sermons and it was brand new. I read the

complete manuscript several days in advance with the preacher's emendations inserted in his own handwriting. Fosdick's manuscript was notable for short sentences and strong, simple English verbs. They were words and sentences that could be spoken with unmistakable meaning. Adjectives were used sparingly, and none was used when the noun carried its own weight of meaning. The big congregation loved it; for the older persons, who had been brought up on stirring sermons, it was a profound emotional experience.

The congregation of churchgoers in the auditorium included several thousand older persons, the generation that remembers Fosdick's ringing golden voice opening the Sunday afternoon National Vesper Hour: "Behold, I stand at the door, and knock." From the press box it was fascinating to see the rapture of those men and women who had seen their traditional faith rise and fall and rise again. As Fosdick had quoted Matthew Arnold in his little book *The Meaning of Faith,* they could remember when "the sea of faith was once, too, at the full."

Several hundred ministers were presented to Fosdick at an informal reception before the Reformation Day service. Their churches represented the full range of Protestant and Eastern Orthodox belief and practice. The famous guest of honor was received with warmth and enthusiasm. In the eyes and memory of this gathering of both conservative and liberal, he was an image of the dignity of preaching and the right of the clergy to be heard. Fosdick was a doughty old champion of their common cause, and they were happy to honor him.

Living by faith in God in a difficult time was Fosdick's favorite pulpit theme and finest personal achievement. So engagingly did he preach this theme, straight out of the Psalms, that in thirty years I heard more quotations from Fosdick's sermons and books, with or without giving him credit, than from any dozen other ministers. Even fundamentalists who made a career of denouncing Fosdick's Modernism were caught repeating his felicitous speech and retelling his inspiring illustrations. South-

ern Baptist and Southern Presbyterian pastors used his little
devotional books at week-night prayer meetings—they deplored
his theology, but his courageous spirit was fetching.

The dates in Harry Emerson Fosdick's long career are important to an understanding of his influence on Protestant
preaching. He was ordained to the Northern Baptist ministry
in 1903, and was a popular preacher from his very first sermons
in Montclair, New Jersey. He appeared on the religious scene
when preaching in the established churches was never stuffier
—it was prescribing nineteenth-century clichés and bromides
to the elect. Fosdick's independence and charm outlasted them
all.

Fosdick blossomed early and bore fruit well into old age. His
best-loved book, *The Meaning of Prayer,* was published in
1915, early in the war that was to bring him to his deepest
moral and spiritual crisis. He was a professor at Union Theological Seminary from 1915 to 1946 and minister of the Riverside Church from 1926 until his retirement in 1946. He became
the leading spokesman of Modernism in the 1920s, and had a
year to go at the Riverside Church when the first atom bomb
was dropped on Hiroshima. His sermons and books reflected
the shattering changes for Christian faith and church life of
the first half of the present century. A New York colleague of
Fosdick's said of him, "He buried the patricians and baptized
the modernists."

Now closer to ninety years than eighty, Fosdick lives in
Bronxville, New York, and is still active in liberal causes in
nearby New York City. He never drove an automobile or locked
his apartment door, and during the Depression he kept his own
income to five thousand dollars a year out of compassion for
his fellow countrymen in the breadlines.

It is easy for the present generation of preachers and laymen
to forget how much American Protestantism owes to Harry
Emerson Fosdick's courage, skill, and grace. He himself was
a casualty to fundamentalism only once—when he lost his New
York Presbyterian pulpit in the storm over the Virgin Birth.

When Bryan and Darrow were fencing over the Tennessee anti-evolution law, Fosdick went to Harvard University as guest preacher, and the college chapel could not hold the congregation of students, most of whom—except for the handful of divinity students—had not been to church since they came to Cambridge.

Fosdick's most famous public declaration was, "I will not bless another war." He was about midway in his pulpit career when he turned this corner. He was one of hundreds of clergymen who came out pacifists from a bloodletting whose promise of peace with honor turned to ashes. And this mass conversion to pacifism was the most dramatic chapter in the story of preachers from 1901 to 1965 until the civil rights struggle of 1963.

In World War I the churches joined the American Red Cross and the Y.M.–Y.W.C.A. in the national effort; many preachers, from bishops to village parsons, became unofficial recruiting sergeants—in their flag-waving sermons, religion and patriotism were one word. Like a mighty army moved the church of God. But not the next time around. Or the next. The clergy drew up its own declaration of independence, in Fosdick's words, and stuck to its guns through World War II and the McCarthy era.

For more than forty years Harry Emerson Fosdick's familiar voice was out front in the never-ending battle for freedom to read the Bible with intelligence and honesty, for freedom of the pulpit, for freedom of thought and speech and conscience for the clergy and their teachers.

But Fosdick was a preacher by trade and a propagandist by avocation. His finest sermons and most eloquent writing were on a single theme. It was neither freedom for man's mind nor social justice nor war and peace. It was the power and the glory of the human spirit under adversity—how to live by faith in a difficult time. In hundreds of sermons from his pulpit or on the air, in many places in every book he has written, he rang the changes on this biblical theme. And who heard him? Men and women who had quit going to church; college students who packed their chapels to hear again what they had heard all their lives in Sunday school and church; lonely farm couples; frustrated and debt-ridden city dwellers; patients in hospitals and the forgotten people in institutions of charities and churches and government. If they ever went to church, they had heard it all before but not with the conviction in this preacher's voice and manner.

When Ralph W. Sockman landed in New York City in 1917 to assume his first and only pastorate, the city was already known throughout Protestantism as "the graveyard of pulpit rhetoric." The editor of a New York church journal once rattled off for me a list of prominent pulpit names, big names from the hinterlands and from England and Scotland, who invaded Manhattan behind glowing build-ups in the church press, all of whom flunked out in New York after a few years. New York was the place where the established denominations maintained their boards and societies and propaganda mills. But far from a stronghold of the Reformation in population. For a preacher coming from a community where Protestants ruled the roost, preaching in New York was like trying to attract and hold a congregation in Grand Central Station or the Waldorf-Astoria lobby. Ralph Sockman lasted forty-four years in one uptown pulpit and thirty-four years on a national radio program.

Sockman at seventy-five has retired from Christ Church, Methodist, his only pastorate. That imposing edifice was dedicated free of debt (the Methodist Church rule) at the bottom of the Depression. Sockman's forty-four-year tour of pulpit duty, like Fosdick's, brackets most of the difficult years of our national church life.

He has also retired from the National Radio Pulpit. Before he was able to tape his radio broadcast, Sockman had to follow a man-killing schedule. He described it to me in an interview during a week in Lent when he was preaching to overflow congregations in downtown St. Louis Christ Church Cathedral. "I had to go to the studio every Sunday morning. The broadcast was at 10:05 A.M. A taxi driver picked me up at 9:40 to take me to Radio City, where an elevator starter had an elevator waiting. The program ended at 10:30, and I took a waiting taxi back uptown to Christ Church. I had just twenty minutes to shift into my regular service and sermon."

I have listened to radio broadcasts of religious services in at least twenty states. A few of the national programs, like the National Radio Pulpit, are first-rate in content and professional in performance—like Ralph Sockman. In metropolitan areas, except in some Southern states and in the Far West, there are fair-to-good programs sponsored by the local church council or by a national denomination. Yet even in these favorable areas, in most broadcasts the preacher gives the impression that he is diluting his message to reach a common denominator of interest. As for the small-town broadcasts of Sunday services and early morning weekday devotions, it is a "vast wasteland" of huckstering, biblical illiteracy, and bigotry multiplied by the air waves.

On a recent Sunday morning, between early breakfast and church hour, I twirled my radio dial for samples of five religious broadcasts, all in the Middle West. The locations ran from towns of twenty-five hundred to small cities of a hundred thousand. It was a painful experience. The level of preaching and music, of prayer and exhortation and begging for contributions, was shamefully low. Three of the five sermons were on the Second Coming—signs and portents that the end of a wicked world is near. The books of Daniel and Revelation were used as calendars. One sermon from a town in Missouri was on juvenile delinquency, which was blamed on mothers who play bridge, smoke cigarettes, and serve cocktails. Another sermon was an attack on the United States Supreme Court for "driving God out of the schools." The preachers I heard that day on the air were as scandalmongering in their prayers as in their preaching; God got an earful.

Friends in the radio business say that this complimentary "service to religion" is the bane of their lives but insist they can do nothing about it—"churches and preachers have influence."

Ralph Sockman's sermons were distinguished in several ways:

the aptness and naturalness of his text (no verbal tricks); completeness of the sermon structure; the swift march of the argument (he had eighteen minutes on radio); the use of homely illustrations from everyday life; and the use of familiar words to establish or sharpen new meanings. Sockman's vernacular was as familiar in Kankakee and Wichita as in New York.

Sockman had another professional knack which perhaps as much as anything else explains his remarkable career: he had a genius for reading the lay mind, its dogging questions and worries. He could see the inside of American family life, and the inside of business and professional and college and community life. He also had a tender streak of irony in his well-stocked mind that is extremely rare in the clergy. It established immediate and responsive contact, for the average American man carries in the back of his mind an ironic image of himself —"I'm not so hot." It is a form of sanity which maturity bestows. Ralph Sockman's sophisticated style would have been unthinkable in the first decade of this century.

Bishop Ivan Lee Holt spent many years in church administration and interdenominational affairs, but his first love was always the pulpit. I first heard him preach in 1911 when he was the very young minister of University Methodist Church, St. Louis, which he founded. Fifty-one years later I heard him deliver a sermon on the first chapter of First Peter to one of the largest congregations in the Middle West. A southerner by birth and upbringing, he was for twenty years pastor of historic St. John's Methodist Church, St. Louis, a record at the time for a Methodist pastorate.

Bishop Holt is the most widely traveled churchman since John R. Mott. He was a founder of both the National and World Councils of Churches and served as president of the old Federal Council of Churches for two years, 1935 and 1936. In 1964, at the age of seventy-eight, Bishop Holt was an observer at the Second Vatican Council in Rome.

Most of the ministers under his supervision did not share his liberal views on the Bible and social problems—a predicament

shared by his friend and colleague Bishop William Scarlett of
the St. Louis diocese of the Protestant Episcopal Church and
by Cardinal Joseph E. Ritter of the St. Louis Catholic archdiocese. In the same line, the Reformed Jewish clergy, as every
journalist in religion finds, is far more liberal than its constit-
uency. In the total area of the American religious structure, the
picture is often of the general far out in front of his reluctant
army. This makes good stories for the news media but is not
calculated to promote peace and harmony.

Bishop Holt is distinguished for his contributions in three
areas of church life marked by controversy. He was president
of the Federal Council of Churches at a time when it was under
heavy fire from conservative Protestant laymen and clergy
across the country, Bishop Holt was one of a handful of high-
placed churchmen who saved the old council from destruction
until it could be merged in 1950 as part of the new National
Council of Churches, which, in its turn, now carries on under
the same attacks. Bishop Holt took the fight to save the Federal
Council into the strongholds of the opposition—luncheon clubs,
business groups, even the private offices of the financial and
industrial tycoons. He had the advantage of being better informed on the hot issues than the critics. He also enjoyed another advantage. Leaders of the opposition found it awkward
to oppose him, for he was a patrician too—in appearance and
bearing and his cultivated speech.

During the Depression I heard Bishop Holt deliver to large
congregations half a dozen sermons that were powerful in
defense of social justice, brotherhood, charity, and mercy. An
authority on the Old Testament prophets, his exposition of their
social teaching in contemporary terms was the very best I ever
heard. In this touchy field also, he enjoyed a personal advantage
in preaching to the reluctant conservative laity, for he took a
sophisticated view of the individual Christian in his complex
modern relationships with society. Holt was never tagged as a
Social Gospeler, or as belonging to any school of theology or
biblical interpretation.

A third area in which Bishop Ivan Lee Holt distinguished himself was in the prolonged, sometimes stormy negotiations, that led in 1939 to the creation of the Methodist Church by a merger of the Methodist Episcopal Church, North, the Methodist Episcopal Church, South, and the Methodist Protestant Church. In this history-making movement for Protestant unity —healing a breach that had been opened in 1845 over the issue of slavery—Bishop Holt was in a fortunate position to exercise patience, foresight, and sweet reasonableness. As a Southerner stationed in a border state, he had hundreds of Methodist friends on both sides of the border. He had been elected bishop of the Methodist Church, South, a year before the united church was formed.

The large First Methodist Church in Evanston, Illinois, was filled in nave and gallery fifteen minutes early; latecomers occupied as many chairs as there was room for. It was a hot June day before air conditioning became general. The big congregation was unique because it included a large number of university professors of science; many of them hadn't been to church since they were sophomores in college until Ernest Fremont Tittle came to Evanston.

Also in the congregation were other professors from Northwestern University, and undergraduates and graduate students; students and faculty members from Garrett Biblical Institute, the Methodist seminary in Evanston; schoolteachers by the score from many states who were taking summer studies in Evanston and Chicago; and, of course, members of the church. I interviewed a few of the public-school teachers, and they told me they never missed a sermon by Tittle; the teachers were members of various denominations, many from the South, where they never heard a liberal like Tittle.

What that cosmopolitan congregation heard was an eloquent, closely packed sermon on the moral authority of Jesus Christ—without any reference to the Trinity, the Virgin Birth, or other miracles. It was noticeable that the minister did not slight his formal order of service to spare himself for the delivery of his sermon, though the state of his health called for more prudence.

The late Edward Dowling, S.J., of St. Louis, ex-newspaper reporter, confidant and confessor of newshawks, Catholic and non-Catholic, after he had suffered a coronary attack, said, "When you have had a coronary like mine, every day is a curtain call." Well, every Sunday in Ernest Fremont Tittle's last years was a curtain call. He was one of those gifted men who drive themselves beyond their physical endurance, crack up, then find their second wind, and go out in a blaze of glory. Tittle had suffered a breakdown in mid-career, a collapse of nerve and will and a deterioration of the heart muscle. He told friends, "I will never be able to preach again." But he recovered a passable measure of health and all of his spirit and returned to his pulpit for many more years—the finest years of his life. Because of his heart condition he was forbidden by his physician to take stairs, so a ramp was built from his study door to the pulpit. He was found lying dead on his church study floor, the page proofs of his last book in his hand.

The Methodist Church has never acknowledged its debt to Tittle for his contribution to the Church's reputation for intellectual honesty. He made religion respectable, at least debatable, in places like university campuses where it was believed smart to believe nothing beyond the horizon. In the national battle between science and religion, modernism and fundamentalism, Tittle was a major figure on the side of freedom and reason. His influence on the clergy was widespread.

Tittle, throughout a long career in both sermons and books, was celebrated as a national spokesman of the Social Gospel and also as a Christian philosopher knowledgeable in the Bible and faith and doctrine. At Evanston, on the edge of a great university campus which is part of an extensive metropolitan area—an area where the conflicts between orthodoxy and modernism have always been sharp—Tittle's hard work was cut out for him: he had to preach to the skeptical, disillusioned educated mind of his postwar generation. He knew when he climbed to his high pulpit that about a third of the people facing him had come to church with the thought that they had left religion behind; religion was for Catholics and the poor Protestant congregations down in the city. They were merely curious to hear what this noted preacher and writer could say that would make any difference. Congregations like that come to church not to be converted—least of all to repent of their sins and turn over a new leaf—but to reflect upon simpler, happier times when their minds were at peace.

On this very modern frontier for Christian faith, Tittle preached about the moral and spiritual problems whose proximity and devilment could not be brushed off. For example, why should the little man be honest when the news was filled with stories of luxury and pleasure paid for by loot, bribery, and plain and fancy thievery? Where was the theologian's "ground of being" for chastity and human kindness? Was it not more sensible to cash in on the profits and wages of arms than to worry about the statesman's everlasting talk about "peace from strength"?

In Tittle's long day, not only wars and peacemaking but the Depression had heavy impact on the content and tone of preaching. The main-line denominations were divided over the Social Gospel, and Tittle was tagged as a Social Gospeler. The fear of communism aggravated the crisis, and the emotion of fear was shamelessly exploited by those Americans opposed to social and economic reform. Tittle's home ground, the Greater Chicago area, was a hotbed of political reaction. In such an atmosphere the liberal clergyman was perpetually under fire. Ernest Fremont Tittle shortened his life and made his last years precarious and painful by intense concentration on his controversial prophetic ministry. His voice for reason and justice and righteousness was silenced only by death.

When L. P. Jacks, noted English Unitarian preacher, professor of philosophy and principal of Manchester College, Oxford, came to Harvard University a few years after World War I to give a series of lectures, he was the gloomiest prophet of religion the young men in the Divinity School had ever heard—that is, in public address. In conversation and bull sessions before the big fireplace in the seminary lounge, Jacks was fun. His public lectures sounded like William Ralph Inge of St. Paul's, London, "the gloomy dean."

Jacks was a penitent figure in a vicarious way. His own country had taken terrible punishment and irretrievable losses in the war. A generation of young men was wiped out, and Jacks bore the marks of sorrow. Many of his students and former students had been slain in war. Many of his friends had lost all their sons, as many as three or four from some families.

Jacks found in the United States a different atmosphere. The League of Nations was already a dead issue. The country was angry about the foreign loans which were not being paid, and it was piling up domestic debts which the Depression would also make unpayable. President Warren G. Harding was dead, and the scandals of his brief administration were beginning to make front-page news. Prohibition had not brought an end to crime and poverty and corruption. But the "cool" Calvin Coolidge administration saw and spoke of nothing but prosperity and tranquility without end. "The country's greatest asset is common sense," said the President. Couéism was in vogue in this country, as popular as mah jongg, the Chinese domino game with tiles. Émile Coué was a French psychotherapist who had reduced his medical science to autosuggestion, which anybody could practice without a license. His formula—"Day by day, in every way, I am getting better and better"—found a congenial climate in political and religious circles.

In such a carnival of good cheer, L. P. Jacks was much too sober for American taste. Things weren't that bad. Maybe in Europe. Pulpit gloom sounded like radicalism, a dirty word.

The first hall at Harvard reserved for Jacks's talks was much too small, and he was moved to a larger auditorium. Undergraduates, graduate students, faculty members, and ministers from the greater Boston area packed the hall. They heard a quiet, scholarly man who never raised his voice or lifted a hand in gesture; sly wit and humor, no heroics, no fine rhetoric; a master of English understatement. Students from the divinity school had known Jacks only from reading his editorials and book reviews in his *Hibbert Journal*.

But what fascinated the American hearers, and provoked weeks of discussion, was the lecturer's heavy tone. Jacks told how our common religious faith and culture had been damaged by the war. He spoke of "the moral tragedy of a generation that has betrayed its ideals." Students were deeply stirred by the unfamiliar tone. Our national spokesmen never talked like that—our political leaders would as soon have embraced communism in public as confess that America had ever betrayed an ideal. Our statesmen were driven by the national cult to insist that we were always to be found on the side of God and the right, and the preacher had better not forget what was the politician's bread and butter. Almost exactly forty years after L. P. Jacks' visit, our national cult of self-righteousness was given total statement by a very prominent American political personage: "This struggle is a struggle between godless people and the people of God."

Yet in recent years, including 1964, I have heard a tone and style like Jacks's from pulpits and platforms and press: the impression from his Harvard lectures that time was running out for Western Judaeo-Christianity. The stern word of urgency is being heard today from both fundamentalist and modernist pulpits. It has inspired many public statements of the National and World Councils of Churches and the popes.

The loneliest figure in the Harvard Yard when L. P. Jacks called was the dean of the Divinity School, Willard L. Sperry. Although he didn't appear to fit the role, Dean Sperry was the hardest-pressed home missionary in the land, for at Harvard he was leading a rear-guard action in defense of the claims of Christian faith and worship. The same struggle was mounting on the campuses of church-related colleges everywhere except in the Deep South. Old schools of higher learning that had been founded and supported at great sacrifice by the major denominations were suing for separate maintenance. Colleges and universities not already free won their freedom from church ties before the era was over. And many of the institutions left under ostensible church control were in fact free. While the old-line denominations, pioneers in higher education, were tearing themselves apart in disputes over evolution and the Bible miracles, they were losing their historic ground in the intellectual community. The Protestantism of the patricians dominated education as their constituents ruled the political realm. Dean Sperry, son of a denominational college president, lived to see church-related education go secular.

Harvard Divinity School, riven and reduced by the split between Trinitarian and Unitarian Congregationalists, then had only fifty students, though this was twice as many as ten years earlier. It held "poor relation" standing on the three-hundred-year-old campus of the Puritan fathers. The natural sciences, the learned professions (theology excepted), and the new School of Business Administration ruled the roost. An undergraduate could not have given directions to a visitor in search of the Divinity School, the department for whose purpose the university was founded.

Dean Sperry was a large, handsome man of extraordinary gifts who, over many years of service at Harvard, gave the melancholy impression that every class in preaching that appeared before him disappointed his hopes. He was a perfectionist, thoroughly disciplined in mind and habits and intolerant of slovenly thought, particularly intolerant of off-the-cuff speech. How many times, after one of his two-hour sessions on the preparation and delivery of sermons, he would lift his eyes from his notes and say, wearily, "Now I know very well that you're not going to write your sermons."

The dean met once in each semester with a committee of seniors to select a list of ministers who would be invited to speak at vespers. The spokesman for one of those committees objected to confining the list to prominent names: "I suggest that we include a few men who haven't reached the top but still can preach." Dean Sperry crushed him: "That is the greatest argument for mediocrity I've ever heard."

The unhappy truth is that Dean Sperry's polished English was the despair of his students, but he never realized it—or maybe he did!

He was a New England patrician in appearance and bearing, yet kind, warmhearted, and generous in his personal relations with his students. At the end of a lecture, he would often call to his desk some student who was having a hard time paying his way or making grades, and hold him for an hour of counseling and encouragement. I myself could not have stayed in the Divinity School three months, let alone three years, if I had not received the generous practical assistance and the spiritual encouragement of Dean Sperry.

The Divinity School's standing has improved since Dean Sperry's death. Religion has had a comeback at Harvard, at least with the administration. Enrollment has gone up, though few parish ministers are turned out.

Students and vacationing preachers who crossed over to the Back Bay to hear Dean Sperry preach were reminded, if they were so literate, that when he was an early Rhodes scholar at Oxford in 1904, the novels of Henry James were in the London bookstalls. But what really distinguished Dean Sperry's polished sermons from the popular evangelical preaching of his day—today's too—was the total absence of bluff and legerdemain. He was unwilling to give up the intellectual community, and he was incapable of pious fraud. Some of his memorable sermons were on various aspects of the problem of evil: students and teachers found his simple honesty refreshing even though he didn't always come up with comforting answers to the questions they had brought to meeting.

Yet when Dean Sperry gave up his Boston pulpit in 1922 to serve full time as dean of the Divinity School, the *Boston Tran-*

*script* had to say, "It was not until he left us that we realized a great preacher had been in our midst."

Edwin T. Dahlberg, retired minister of Delmar Baptist Church in St. Louis, made the news several times. When he belittled the namby-pamby scruples of many Christians of his day as "Mickey Mouse morals," his remark got circulation wherever church news was printed.

Dahlberg, a big, hearty man, with a voice in proportion, is the son of Scandinavian parents who had settled in northern Minnesota; he was blessed with the rugged constitution of his forebears. The pioneer stock is reflected in his experience and preaching. Dahlberg says that every time he returns to his boyhood home and visits the family plot in the little cemetery, he is startled to read on a child's small stone "Edwin T. Dahlberg." An older brother died in infancy, and when the present prominent minister was born he was given the same name—another Scandinavian custom.

Dahlberg's sermons are filled with wonderful stories of his childhood and youth—he has total recall of both incident and Scandinavian-English idiom. He and a sister and brother attended high school in a town twelve miles from their home, and during the school week they did light housekeeping in rented rooms above a store. Minnesota winters are long and cold and snow-banked. Long before daylight, every Monday morning the father took the three children to town in the farm wagon, loaded with cured meat, eggs, milk and butter, potatoes, beans, cereals, home-baked bread, and pastry. The father called for his children on Friday afternoon and they would then spend a busy weekend taking a hand with the chores and helping their mother prepare the next week's provisions for their five school days. It was a rugged life, but the experience stood Edwin Dahlberg in good stead when, as president of the National Council of Churches, he spent the Christmas holidays with American armed forces in Alaska.

During his long St. Louis pastorate, Dahlberg served three stormy years as president of the National Council of Churches,

1957 to 1960. In those three years his mail disclosed a depth
and breadth of bigotry that would have been devastating to a
man of smaller faith. Hate was nationally organized and lushly
financed, and it was open season on the liberal clergy.

A pacifist from his theological seminary days, champion of
the underprivileged, and outspoken on any issue that appeals to
his conscience, Dahlberg has been in the middle of as many
controversies as any American churchman in this century.

He has faced conflicts of opinion in his own congregations
too. In his St. Louis community Dahlberg was assailed for his
stand in favor of civil rights and against the color line in
churches. A prominent Baptist layman, at his country club one
Saturday evening, said, "I'll return to church when that nigger
lover is out of the Delmar pulpit." This remark would not
represent the spirit of the Delmar congregation, however. All
five of Dahlberg's churches have stood unitedly and loyally
behind him.

Most religious news editors would agree that Edwin Dahlberg has been one of the two or three most influential Protestant
spokesman in a decade. As pastor and national church officer
he held the esteem of strong men who disagreed violently with
his views and policies. He plucked from the clash of opinion
the barb of personal animosity, and he did this by forbearance
and love, for he is the gentlest of men.

# 8

# A President Dies . . .

1901. On the fifth of September, 1901, my father came riding home from town after dark, bringing the news that President William McKinley had been shot at the Pan-American Exposition in Buffalo, New York, by a foreigner with an unpronounceable name. Father ran the hardware store for the town's richest man and was unable to get away earlier.

First word of the shooting in Buffalo was picked up by the telegraph operator at the Illinois Central railroad depot. He made a copy of the message and handed it to one of the loafers in the depot, who ran uptown, waving the little piece of yellow paper and spreading the news by word of mouth as he ran. All business halted as if an earthquake had struck. Townspeople and farmers came together in small groups, men and women separately, to talk about the awful crime—it was assumed by everybody that our handsome and beloved President would die. He lived until September 14.

On our fifty-acre farm two and a half miles from town we had no telephone and no rural mail delivery. So we had to wait for father to bring the news. Mother and the five children at home gathered in the dining room while father ate his late supper by lamplight; the rest of us had eaten earlier. A big picture of President McKinley hung on the dining-room wall, which was papered with newspapers; father was a Republican county and township worker, and he had brought the picture home from the 1900 campaign.

The family scene in the shadowy dining room was like a funeral; my older sister Nellie, nineteen, wept. But I think father was the one most deeply moved by sorrow. He was a Union army veteran like President McKinley, and the emotional ties of the Grand Army of the Republic were passionate. All of us, however, felt that we had lost a noble friend and benefactor. The President was a Methodist, too; he was superintendent of the Methodist Sunday school in Canton, Ohio, his home town when he was governor of the state. We knew his life story well, and he was our ideal of what a President should be.

Father did his best to answer our flood of questions, but he really knew no more of the details of the crime than the telegram carried. We had to wait for the next day's newspaper for a full account: the gracious President holding a public reception; the anarchist Leon Czolgosz concealing his little pistol under a handkerchief. The family followed Father into the living room and took chairs while he read a Bible lesson—an every-night observance—then we knelt on the rag carpet for his prayer.

The assassination of President McKinley was the subject of the next Sunday-school session and preaching service at our country church. Our young woman schoolteacher at the district school held a program of mourning, with Bible lesson and prayer, and a few of the children were asked to express their feelings.

1923. When President Warren G. Harding died suddenly in his San Francisco hotel room in 1923, Harvard University, always a stickler for the proprieties, held a memorial service. Professor Kirsopp Lake of the Divinity School, a clergyman of the Church of England (which later unfrocked him), delivered the memorial address.

"The young will say, 'What a pity! A man is taken off at the peak of his career and in the prime of life, when he holds the highest office in his country.'

"And the old will say, 'What an easy way to die!'"

The service at Harvard was purely ceremonial. The national period of mourning was not much different. The state funeral was a pageantry of decent respect for the nation's chief executive whose term had been cut short—the pomp and ceremony were as much for the office as for the man.

During his low-voltage campaign, Harding's special train stopped at Union Station, St. Louis, and the candidate and his wife walked to the tall iron fence which divides the train shed from the great concourse. The candidate introduced himself and his wife to the crowd behind the fence by saying, "We're just folks," and his simple remark became a campaign slogan, more important than his few speeches on the issues. And when he was dead, the state addresses and the sermons and prayers emphasized that he was "a man of the people, with the common touch."

By August 1923, when President Harding died, rumors of scandals in his administration were already spreading, although the worst was yet to come. His strange entourage of appointees and playmates, the little coterie of hard-drinking, gambling men, gave public opinion an uneasy feeling. The clergy was becoming critical. Much of the gossip was wild and irresponsible.

But more was involved in the self-conscious mourning for a President. By the time we reached President Harding's death, skepticism had set in—an agonizing period of self-examination that lasted until Pearl Harbor. Disappointment with the war and with the Wilson peace and in the new administration was the source of this infection. It was a trial of faith for a generation that had not yet identified and buried all its dead from a crusade for freedom. Hundreds of sermons were preached on the subject of national honor and the image of American idealism.

1945. Late on the afternoon of Thursday, April 12, 1945, the radio networks interrupted their broadcasts to announce that President Franklin D. Roosevelt had died suddenly at "The Little White House," his cottage at Warm Springs, Georgia. This watering place and national treatment center for polio victims was his favorite retreat and vacation spot.

I had gone off duty at the old *St. Louis Star-Times*, where my wartime rewrite job started at 6 A.M., and was among six or eight men, neighbors from my old St. Louis South Side, gathered in a barber shop. I shall never forget the serious talk of our little group after our first stunned reaction to the news. We included a few workingmen, two salesmen, a couple of old retired men, besides the four barbers.

"Another war casualty," was the first comment I heard. And I heard the same remark, with variations, many times during that long weekend of national mourning, in the newsroom, on streetcars and buses, and in eating places. Throughout the whole Western world, in newspapers and news magazines and on radio, President Roosevelt's death drew the same comment in words and cartoons. I also heard a second theme emphasized in memorial services in churches: a tribute to the late President's devotion to duty under the handicap of his lameness and failing health.

There was another element in the national mourning, and it swelled in importance and emphasis as the days went by—a profound concern for the new President, Harry S. Truman. Although Truman had been in the United States Senate since 1934, he had been Vice-President less than three months and was not well known; he had been completely overshadowed by the wartime President. Thousands of prayers were spoken for the man from Missouri who had been so suddenly thrust into the nation's highest office. There were many sermons and addresses on "the inscrutable ways of God's providence."

Today, twenty years after the event, it seems strange that the American people were taken so completely by surprise by the news of President Roosevelt's death, for they had seen, in news pictures, and heard—and ignored—a sober warning: a sick and wasted and weary President addressing Congress from his wheel chair in the well of the House of Representatives on March 1; he was reporting to Congress and the nation on the recent Summit Conference at Yalta.

It was wartime, and President Roosevelt's funeral was, of course, curtailed in pomp and ceremony by the grim circumstances. The train bearing his body arrived at Union Station, Washington, D.C., Saturday morning, April 14, and the funeral procession moved slowly through the streets to the White House. This public occasion, rather than the formal funeral and burial services, was the high mark of the national mourning. The streets of the nation's capital were lined with thousands of people who were paying silent tribute to the man who had been their leader during the Depression years and now for four years, their captain in war.

Bishop Angus Dun of the Episcopal Church diocese of Washington conducted the funeral service in the East Room of the White House. There was no eulogy. That night the President's body was taken by train to Hyde Park, New York, where Sunday morning Franklin D. Roosevelt was buried in a garden plot on the family estate.

The national feeling of sorrow and loss was sharpened and deepened by the ordeal of war—the people would again be taken by surprise when the war in Europe ended in less than a month; Germany surrendered on May 7. At various memorial services, I heard comment on the fate which took the country's war leader so near the end of the terrible struggle.

1963. It is three o'clock on Saturday morning, November 23, 1963. Men and women are kneeling in a light rain on the steps of St. Patrick's Cathedral on Fifth Avenue, New York City; the doors of the cathedral are locked. Parishioners and visitors have been coming and going since two o'clock on the previous afternoon, beginning as soon as they heard the news of the assassination of President John F. Kennedy in Dallas. They came to pray for the soul of their youngest President, the first

Roman Catholic President, and for his family, their country, and themselves. Men and women weep on the streets, in the subways, in front of their television sets.

The late November 1963 period of mourning was not purely ceremonial; it drew more participants, more watchers and listeners than any other event in the nation's history. Millions of Protestants and Jews followed the broadcasts and telecasts of Cardinal Cushing's Requiem Mass. And they followed the unruly progress of the riderless horse. Sunday's melodrama in the Dallas jail was profoundly shocking to the nation's image of itself.

Roving reporters interviewed men and women on the street, in bars and eating places, in lines before movie houses, and their comments were more revealing of national feeling than all the eulogies. Many of the persons interviewed were pious; they said what they had been taught to say in Sunday school and church. But for more of them it was skepticism that provided all the relief there was to be had from a spectacle of horror. The assassination of President Kennedy was a terrible event, but it was senseless, wanton, and these plain citizens could see no Providence in it.

I attended worship at the Cathedral Church of St. John the Divine on November 24, 1963. The preacher was the Canon Sacrist Edward N. West. Every minister knows that his most difficult pulpit task is the sermon for a special occasion. The subject is assigned, and it is of public concern. The people come to church, many of them for the first time in months, with an idea in their minds of what they should hear. On that mournful Sunday in November the mood of the worshipers was not for listening to a man's words except as they reflected their own thoughts.

Canon West's sermon met the occasion with dignity and plain speech. As in thousands of pulpits that day, his subject was the national harvest of hate, the evil in men's hearts, and the need for repentance. I have heard John Donne's famous

"No man is an Iland" in dozens of sermons, but never did it fall so naturally into place.

This stated service of the church in the name of the state is as old as religion or government. There is no more settled American tradition than the right and duty of the clergy to participate in public functions. In this public sense, religious faith is an Establishment even in a democracy. No matter what the Supreme Court or Congress may ordain, the ceremonial function of religion on behalf of the state is not likely to change. The practice requires no law to support it.

# PART TWO

PART TWO

# 9

# The Battle of the Books

In the early 1900s a favorite with evangelical congregations was a hymn written by Isaac Watts in 1707: "Alas, and did my Saviour bleed?" No beetle-browed theologian ever wrote a plainer statement of the faith of our fathers.

> Alas, and did my Saviour bleed?
> And did my Sovereign die?
> Would He devote that sacred head
> For such a worm as I?

The old hymn has undergone two successive alterations during the period covered by this book. Both are significant for the change they reveal in the religious climate.

The vermicular last line was just too much for the busy, busy, cheerful Christians who were about to convert the heathen world, and for whom at home in a nation already under God the saints were eating high on the hog. It was discouraging to compel any man to call himself a worm. Man was no worm; at the worst he was only a reluctant disciple of peace and good will. Was he not building a brave new world? Accordingly, the editors of the hymnbooks rewrote the offending line from Watts. Instead of "For such a worm as I?" it read, "For such an one as I?" (Try and sing that spinsterish phrase and make it music!)

Then, after the Christian world had won the war to end war, another war came, the like of which the whole world had never seen, for destruction of life and gear and nasty hangover, in which old allies became enemies and old enemies new allies. Mussolini and Stalin and Hitler had emerged—all out of Christian upbringing, too. Buchenwald. Hiroshima. Missionaries had been routed from posts held by Christian forces for more than a century.

The editors of hymnbooks were impressed—like the poor wretch who suddenly realized he was going to be hanged Friday—"and here it is Wednesday." The offending line was rewritten once more. In the hymnbooks of 1963 it reads, "For sinners such as I?"

Hymn-singing Christians of the Western world are sinners again, if not actually worms. This much they admit.

What happened to the old hymns happened in theology, too. A pitiless spotlight was thrown on man's split-level nature and his sorry history. He got what the physicians call heroic treatment. Even his Sunday-go-to-meeting piety was suspect. The new image of man in the eyes of God was no longer the deacon in morning coat and spats but the old Adam in sackcloth and ashes.

The new theology was a blend of Augustine, Calvin, Edwards, Spengler, and Freud. It held out hope but warned that it would be fulfilled too late to be enjoyed. The new theology was also very learned, right out of the books, all of which means it is harder to preach than any creed come down in archaic speech and hymns—the Lord only knows how many American congregations could testify to this handicap on a popular pulpit.

The new day in doctrine and preaching was a return to a study in depth of Paul's Letter to the Romans—as with Martin Luther and John Wesley. It all started from a book written before World War II—Karl Barth's famous *Commentary on Romans*. (Before this book was translated into English, I used to go a year at a time and never hear a sermon on Romans except on the comforting chapter eight.)

Now it would be absurd to say that there was no preaching of orthodoxy or biblical theology between, say, 1880 and 1944. There were the German-language churches, but these conservative, liturgical bodies were outside the mainstream of Protestant church life. They were outside community life, too. Denominations with colonial backgrounds reaped nothing but sorrow from preaching doctrine; the small minority that was interested invariably fell out among themselves, and there were heresy hunts and divided congregations. The Northern Presbyterians decided to enforce doctrinal purity but succeeded only in splitting their denomination, which became static for a generation.

It was the old Evangelical Synod of North America, now part of the United Church of Christ, that gave to American Protestantism its most important theologian since Jonathan Edwards. It was Reinhold Niebuhr who made the cheerio "ever onward and upward" preaching of the prewar years sound foolish.

Niebuhr's attacks on the Social Gospel—its unfounded optimism and one-sided emphasis—were discussed in Chapter 3. But that was a by-product of his general stand on theology; it was his theology that was fundamental to the battle of the books. Niebuhr himself never compromised his demand for justice and measures for human welfare. He remained a Christian Socialist. His books on doctrine, philosophy, biblical interpretation, and history established his reputation by shaking the Establishment to its foundations. What he said in praise of God and dispraise of man was a profound shock to theological seminaries and popular pulpits. Niebuhr made it more difficult for the rest of the clergy to repeat optimistic platitudes; his own preaching gave the effect of a consummate ease.

For his brethren in the ministry, Niebuhr opened the Scriptures anew; he made them reread their New Testament and history. He made pastors take another long, hard look at their well-behaved, comfortable congregations.

People who had read Niebuhr's books or heard his lectures but had never heard him preach were in for a happy and stimulating surprise. He started out as a pastor and always loved to preach. He was a "natural" in the pulpit, where his big frame towered and his splendid voice and clear enunciation were impressive and delightful. Niebuhr read his lectures but delivered his sermons from a few notes.

He came to St. Louis to give a series of five midday sermons during one week in Lent. The services were held in a downtown cathedral, and there were standees at every service. The sermon was limited to twenty minutes. This didn't matter, not with a preacher like Niebuhr. His sermons on sin and grace and forgiveness and reconciliation were deeply moving. The congregation included a large crowd of preachers from many denominations, and after hearing him every day they remarked on his diction, his change of pace and his emphasis, and of course the perfect construction of the sermons. And the great man had wit. How many times in my rounds of the churches as a professional journalist have I sat in my pew, closed my eyes, and prayed to God to give the man in the pulpit just one tiny grain of the salt of humor!

Niebuhr was the speaker at a breakfast meeting of clergy from Midwestern states during a week's convocation at the Chicago Theological Seminary. Several of the ministers were his former students at Union Theological Seminary, and several others were his old friends from the years when he was a pastor. He startled them all. Niebuhr began his informal remarks in that bass growl of his lighter moments, yet apparently in deadpan seriousness: "Preachers must not expect their people to really like them. They may admire you, look up to you, they will probably support you loyally. But they won't really like you. For people just don't like the man who stands up before them, above reply, and reads them moral lectures."

A few of Niebuhr's listeners took his remarks as a joke and laughed. But some were offended—I heard their objections afterward.

I recall that at the time I thought it quite possible the famous theologian was pulling the legs of his brethren among the clergy; I knew he enjoyed a good joke, especially fun at the expense of pomposity. But, since that day over thirty years ago, I have visited too many churches, watched and heard too many earnest ministers in action, to fail to appreciate Niebuhr's point. Now I know he was not kidding anybody, for pomposity is an occupational disease among the clergy, and it is all too easy for seriousness to overdo itself, to pass into a boring posture. Imitators of Niebuhr's style give their congregations a bad half-hour: with them, the salt has lost *his* savor.

The enormous vogue of Reinhold Niebuhr among the *cognoscente* did not mean that fundamentalist theology was discarded by the mass of clergy and the masses of the faithful. Far from it. There are more fundamentalists in American churches today than when Niebuhr started writing over thirty years ago, and nobody understands this theological lag better than he. The fundamentalist churches have grown much faster than the old established bodies with their theological seminaries tied to secular universities where Niebuhr was heard and read. He disturbed the liberals, who were used to it and could take it.

Martin Niemöller must reflect many times upon the inscrutable ways of Providence in guiding his career as a Christian preacher and churchman. This German citizen and church president has made himself a familiar and beloved figure in the United States. Commander of a German submarine in World War I, noted pastor of a fashionable church in a Berlin suburb, outspoken anti-Nazi and for seven years an inmate of Nazi prisons, Niemöller became a Christian pacifist after World War II. If a record like that wouldn't make a man a controversial figure, what would? Niemöller has preached hundreds of sermons in this country, and calls many American church people by their first names.

When Niemöller made his first visit to the United States in 1947, after his release from concentration camp in 1945, he was a dramatic figure of the war, with his prison pallor and careworn face and haunted eyes. He addressed an interchurch gathering of eleven thousand persons in the St. Louis municipal auditorium on the meaning of Luther's Reformation for the modern church. In an interview, Niemöller told me how he had taught himself English from textbooks brought to his prison cell—"I had to do something with my mind to keep from going crazy." At the time he had, of course, no idea that he would ever have occasion to use his self-taught English with American audiences. His first American sermons were in bookish English. But when he returned to the United States in 1952, he spoke the borrowed language like a native and had even mastered American slang.

Niemöller is quite at home in the new postwar theology and the writings of Karl Barth and Niebuhr, and his preaching reflects it. His expository sermons over a period of more than fifteen years were models of that exceedingly difficult and long-neglected art. They balanced theology with social concern. Best remembered were his short sermons on the Psalms, the parables of Jesus, and passages from the Epistles.

Niemöller is a controversial figure in his homeland; his running feud with Karl Barth over the issue of the relationship between church and state has been fully covered in American church journals. We have the same hot issue over here, only in a more advanced stage. Niemöller is a controversial person in the United States, too. This came out in his informal talks before large groups of clergy. The conservative ministers, who were a majority, approved of Niemöller's biblical theology but looked upon him as a radical Socialist in his political views; they admired his pacifism but rejected it.

In the presence of Martin Niemöller, who understands European power politics inside out, and asking him loaded questions from inadequate knowledge, the ministers were not aware that they were exposing themselves—it was as if they were standing in front of a fluoroscope. Niemöller was having the time of his life. The conservative clergy went away unhappy because they had been unable to lead their famous guest to praise the West as being the Christian side in the cold war and to denounce the East without reservation. But Niemöller was critical of both East and West. And he was brilliant in the give-and-take.

The overriding impression carried away from Niemöller's meetings was that most American ministers reflect the opinions of the most conservative members of the American press; they are out of sympathy with the national journals of their own denominations. Niemöller served as a lightning rod, attracting the heat and force of clashing views. Of course there were also many clergymen in those meetings who agreed with him.

The National Fellowship of Directors of Christian Education, United Church of Christ, was holding its annual meeting in a St. Louis hotel. The speaker at a sectional meeting was Paul Tillich, noted German-American theologian, a minister of the United Church of Christ. He gave a lecture on "Religion and the Visual Arts," illustrated with slides. Tillich explained that he was speaking as a theologian and a philosopher.

I interviewed Tillich before his lecture and asked him about a paragraph in my printed copy—"Are you going to use this?" He took time to refill his big, low-slung briar pipe and light it. He was not trying to evade my question—not Tillich! He knew what he was going to do. He was searching his mind for the right American idiom. He loves American idiom and has an amazing mastery of its use, for a man who did not know a word of English when he came to this country in 1933 at the age of forty-seven. Finally, he gave me his answer: "Yes, I'm going to use it. Let it stand."

Here is the paragraph, for which Tillich used a Cézanne "Still Life" for illustration:

"About this I must say something which goes back to my earliest encounter with the visual arts immediately after I came out of the ugliness of the First World War and was introduced into modern art by a friend, Dr. Eckhard V. Sydow, who wrote the first book on German expressionism. At that time I came to the conclusion that an apple of Cézanne has more presence of ultimate reality than a picture of Jesus by Hoffman, which can now be found in the Riverside Church of New York City."

After the lecture, I questioned a dozen or more directors of Christian education, twice as many women as men. All the men would say about Tillich's disparagement of the Hoffman face of Christ was, "His comment was interesting." The women showed their hurt feelings—"But Hoffman's picture is beautiful." "It may not be the highest art, but it is reverent, and I shall continue to use it." Two of the younger women were amused by Tillich's remark; they had never used the Hoffman picture since getting their degree in religious education.

In his talk, Tillich said he had "always learned more from pictures than from theological books." Man has tried to express ultimate reality in three general ways, he said. "Two indirect ways are philosophy or metaphysics, and art. The third and direct way we call religion. Here ultimate reality becomes manifest through ecstatic experiences expressed in symbols and myths."

Idealistic art, according to Tillich, is marked by the element of hope "which sees in the present the anticipation of future perfection." Religious art of the expressionist style Tillich called "ecstatic-spiritual. It accepts the individual thing and person but goes beyond it. It is realistic and at the same time mystical. It is restless, yet points to eternal rest."

He had warm praise and appreciation for modern music, poetry, and drama; they expressed one of his key ideas, "the courage to be." He defined this as "the courage to bring into an artistic form the negativities of existence. I think this shows very great courage. Even if they did not do anything else, I would say they did a great thing."

Tillich's sermons are often startling and shocking to congregations that have never heard him before because they begin with a frank and honest discussion of "the negativities of existence"—the cruel paradoxes of life, its injustices and inequalities; the devastating experience of forgiveness, the fear of death which the modern Christian cleverly disguises; the demonic nature of worldly power; the mystery of prayer, which may be ecstatic joy or barren dust in the heart. Paul Tillich is an existentialist preacher, and in this sense he is a European talking out of the background of his own life under "the ugliness of war." His eloquent honesty in dealing with human existence, the tragic sense of life, is missing from most American preaching.

Some of Tillich's sermons and lectures and books shock his American audiences for a different reason than their frank disclosure of the facts of life. Tillich is bracketed with Reinhold Niebuhr as a Christian Socialist, and this gives the fainthearted, decorous deacons and elders chills and fever. Tillich saw the rise of the revolutionary movement of the proletariat in Europe, and when he describes the foundations of that movement, its primary causes and hopes, and its many sympathizers among the clergy and other intellectuals, American churchmen see only a vision of horror—the destruction of property, the triumph of labor unions, bad manners, and a general insolence. The Reverend Dr. Tillich sounds more like a radical than a sound churchman.

But Paul Tillich makes no concessions to the indifferent or hostile listener, and in this respect he is not very modern. In the pulpit he is completely sure of himself, sure of his mastery of his subject and of its importance. He is a big, hearty German-American who loves wine and enjoys life, and his pulpit and platform manner is warm and friendly and sparkling with the charm of wit, as well as impressive with the weight of learning. His congregations know they will be rewarded for paying close attention. Now an old man, Paul Tillich has kept his spirit of youth, a priceless asset in preaching.

Expounding Bible texts and themes is not every man's dish. In too many sermons the argument bogs down in what might be called the fine print at the bottom of the page.

A large and famous church in a seaboard city was filled, as
it is every Sunday, with tourists, students, and other visitors
and the church members. They came to hear a man who is
widely advertised as "the greatest expository preacher of our
time." His subject was a certain character in the Gospels about
whom no more than a hundred words are handed down. The
long sermon was deadly dull and absolutely pointless. Nobody
talked about it at the coffee hour which followed. It was a
melange of domestic trivia, of Galilee frosted with pious senti-
mentalities—an encyclopedia of useless information. If the
worshiper was impressed, he was not edified.

This great church is sustained by the loyalty of three thousand members, by denominational loyalty, and a year-round
daily program of activities and services, professional and volunteer. The Sunday-morning worship service and sermon are only
one among a hundred and one attractions. (In most city
churches, large and small, the religion editor in search of his
story finds that, increasingly, the sermon counts for less and
less.)

The parade of archaic lore is only one kind of bookishness.
Are its ultramodern variants any better? In our mushrooming
suburban oases of prosperity and status, churches seem to place
a premium on verbal gymnastics and vapidity. Sermons have
no cutting edge that might prick an uneasy conscience or balloon of pride. Some I have heard sounded like edited tape
recordings of sessions in pastoral counseling. The language was
a jargon of amateur psychoanalysis plus Pollyanna. A few notes
taken down verbatim:

"The guilt harassments of societal involvement. . . . The self-
revelation of God in the secret chambers of a searching heart.
. . . This mystery bespeaks identification. . . . The lonely spirit
of a man caught up in the loneliness of that spirit whom we
have agreed to call God. . . . The shadow of the Cross pursues
all our self-aggrandizements. . . . The unwearied pilgrim in a
weary world. . . . In the spiritual economy of a forgiving God,
sin is not outgrown, it is outlived. . . . The Resurrection is the

morning star which sings in [spoken as one word] the ecstasy
of eternal spring."

It would be fun to see a national contest arranged to bring
forth new hymns of the Christian faith expressing this gibberish.
In some quarters, at least, we have turned from the Battle of
the Books to a litany of footnotes.

# 10

# Heresy Hunting
# and the American Heritage

"I'm a Baptist born and a Baptist bred, and when I'm gone, I'll be a Baptist dead." Southern Baptists talk more about their denominational loyalty than any other variety of Christians on earth. The Baptist brotherhood is an amazing phenomenon of the spirit, a genuine cooperative movement of more than 32,000 local churches, each a law unto itself. The national convention has no ceded authority; it can only advise. Yet it has been highly successful in carrying on missions, education, evangelism, and benevolence on behalf of its more than ten million members, who are knit together with a strong family feeling. Originating among pioneers in coonskin caps, the Southern Baptists remain a rural people. Even though many of them now comprise big-city congregations, they have not become citified —they remember their origins; the IBM machine hasn't licked them. They represent a proud tradition of American democracy at work in religion and welfare service.

Like the nation itself, the Southern Baptist Convention is still growing, and one of its growing pains is the bedevilment of extremism. They are loners. They observe closed communion and do not join church councils. Along with their informality and evangelistic fervor goes a streak of conservatism. At the extreme, this means aggressive and bigoted ultras who stalk every annual convention and scrutinize every publication in search of leaks in the dam of orthodoxy.

At five of the six conventions I remember best, the moderates from the Southeast, Middle West, and North were in control. But in 1962 at San Francisco, extremists from Southern California and Texas poured into the convention city by train, plane, bus, and car. "The wild men have ganged up on us and we are in trouble," a moderate leader from North Carolina told me.

The year before, Broadman Press had published a scholarly book, *The Message of Genesis*, by Professor Ralph Elliott of Midwestern Baptist Theological Seminary in Kansas City. The Nashville publishing house is operated by the Southern Baptist Sunday School Board. Elliott's interpretation of the Creation story, the Fall, and Noah's Flood reflects a viewpoint that has been commonplace among moderate Protestants for fifty years —not a radical innovation. But the extremists examined the convention registry and, confident of a majority, rallied their votes under the leadership of convention president K. Owen White, pastor of the First Baptist Church in Houston, Texas.

They passed two resolutions. The first affirmed the faith of Southern Baptists in "the entire Bible as the authoritative, authentic, infallible word of God." The second got down to the case at hand: "We express our abiding and unchanging objection to the dissemination of theological views in any of our seminaries which would undermine such faith in the historical accuracy and doctrinal integrity of the Bible, and . . . we courteously request the trustees and administrative officers of our institutions and other agencies to take such steps as shall be necessary to remedy at once those situations where such views now threaten our historic position."

The eight thousand delegates from fifty states knew that "those situations" meant Elliott. The phrase "we courteously request" was a substitution for "we demand"—its framers knew better than to go against the grain of Baptist independence. But once the vote was counted, the ultras were jubilant. Elliott's fate was sealed. He lost his case at the 1963 convention in

Kansas City. He was dismissed from his seminary post and his book was withdrawn from publication.

In 1925, Southern Baptists led in the support of the Tennessee antievolution law that led to the Scopes "monkey trial." Nearly forty years later they were still battling over the "historical accuracy" of the Genesis accounts which scholars regard as prescientific. The accounts themselves disagree, so why shouldn't the Baptists? For seminary professors respected within their profession across denominational lines, it is no joke. Three years afterward, the San Francisco witch hunt has not lost its venom and terror, a sad state of affairs for the pioneer spirit.

The Lutheran Church-Missouri Synod shares one likeness with the Southern Baptists—it is a fast-growing denomination. Otherwise they are almost exact opposites in many ways. The Missouri Synod Lutherans hew to centralism; they are sticklers for a high-church tradition, liturgical, confessional, reserved. And even in a rural parish they preserve the ways of the city. Moreover, until World War I, they were a homogeneous foreign-language group living and worshiping in a very respectable German ghetto.

At the turn of the century, the Lutheran pastor—he was never called minister or preacher—was an American schoolboy's mental picture of the old-fashioned *Bürgermeister*. Hearty and hale from good German food and drink, he subscribed to the St. Louis *Zeitung* and found his entertainment at the Odeon or Liederkranz. When he spoke, it was usually in German and in louder tones than our Methodist minister used except in the pulpit, and he spoke fondly, with a broad accent, of the Fatherland from which he had fled. But what really set him apart from the husbands and fathers in our Methodist world was when he strode down the street in his black suit and black hat, several paces ahead of his wife.

Even today, the world of the Missouri Synod is a man's world, and it is reflected in preaching and pastoral care. Asked about the issue at a convention, one young pastor, my neighbor and friend, said indignantly, "If my church ever permits women to vote in parish meetings, I will resign." His pretty young wife laughed heartily. The Missouri Synod, with more than two and a quarter million members, is one of the few remaining institutions in America where women have no vote, but that does not mean they have no voice.

Sixty years ago, a worthy pastor was not supposed to have any worldly wisdom. His simple trust in the ravens that fed Elijah was what distinguished him from his sensible laymen, for whom good churchmanship was no barrier to bettering their earthly lot. Congregations took delight in a kind of respectful pity for a good man whom they regarded as childlike. And they never heaped him with so many worldly goods as to tempt his heart away from the incorruptible riches he was laying up in heaven.

Today I am well acquainted with many Lutheran pastors who show no lack of worldly wisdom. They are good fun to be with. Their incomes are still low by comparison with the clergy of other denominations. During World War II, I knew men with big families who had a heroic struggle to manage on eighteen hundred dollars a year. They must have leaned heavily on their old-fashioned German habits of thrift.

A healthy regard for the enjoyment of the good Lord's provisions is heard in Lutheran sermons and may be tasted in parish activities—it covers beer and cocktails and port wine and cigars. Brought intact from Europe, this tradition greatly impressed a boy raised in a home-grown American church atmosphere where smoking, drinking, dancing, and card playing were frowned upon. We ate ourselves into a stupor after sitting through three hours of Sunday school and church but were horrified by the elegant *joie de vivre* of our Lutheran and Episcopalian neighbors. When I was in the eighth grade, my mother was shocked to learn that my German Lutheran schoolmate had access to the family icebox, which held more beer than milk. I didn't dare add that my pal feasted me after school every day at the free-lunch counter of his father's saloon.

In those days, the patrician Establishment in our neighborhood in the South Side of St. Louis was represented by a Presbyterian and a Congregational church. The latter, a beautiful stone building that was filled twice each Sunday, flourished until the minister ran for Congress on an anti-Prohibition platform. Both edifices have long since passed into the hands of fundamentalist sects. During the same period, Southern Baptists were moving into the neighborhood like grasshoppers on a Kansas wheat field. Their three large churches in the area include two that are the largest Protestant congregations in the state. As the Baptists swarmed in from the countryside, the Lutherans prospered and moved to the suburbs. The membership of the last remaining Missouri Synod congregation in the neighborhood is a dwindling one.

Social mobility is making for change in the make-up of Missouri Synod churches, and it is not merely the Americanization of the German enclave. I have talked to several married couples who left other communions to join. They praise the beauty and dignity of Lutheran worship, the friendliness of older members at parish functions. More than half the denomination's new members in large and small cities now come from non-Lutheran backgrounds. The mother of two little girls, a former Congregationalist whose husband had been a Catholic, said warmly, "For the first time, my children are really learning the Bible."

In at least a dozen small-town and rural churches of various denominations, I met more than a few older people who listened to the Lutheran Hour on radio every Sunday afternoon. Their own ministers' sermons left them unsatisfied, and they wanted "to hear the Gospel again." Some of them were widows; for them, loneliness and sorrow were the problems of their last years, and they found here comfort which they got nowhere else.

Oswald C. J. Hoffmann is the Lutheran Hour's warmhearted,

vigorous preacher. Like Ralph Sockman, he is a master of the vernacular, freshening old texts with straightforward American idiom—and insight. Preaching on John 18:25, where Peter is asked if he is one of Jesus' disciples, Hoffmann begins: "Self-confidence is the most highly prized virtue of the twentieth century. . . . With complete self-confidence and in full possession of all his self-confident virtues, Simon Peter did just what he boasted he would not do. He walked out on Christ."

Most of Hoffmann's texts are familiar and well worn. He never wrenches a verse out of context or turns it upside down to get attention. He relies on a lively presentation in everyday language, sharpening the familiar idea and driving it home in short words and sentences spoken in a casual, matter-of-fact way. Underneath his relaxed manner, however, there is a fund of professional skill and training. An experienced journalist, Hoffmann served for many years as the Missouri Synod's public-relations director. Others who lack this undergirding and try only for the result often fall into cheap sensationalism or serve up sixty-four-dollar words to express a dime's worth of meaning. Their listeners know the difference.

The strength from which a popular preacher like Hoffmann negotiates the colloquial Gospel is in large part the Missouri Synod tradition of scholarship. They take their doctrines seriously, and this makes for a conservatism not unlike that of the Southern Baptists. Only a couple of weeks after the latter's 1962 convention, the triennial convention of the Lutheran Church–Missouri Synod met in Cleveland, Ohio. The hottest item on the agenda was a charge of heresies against Martin H. Scharlemann, a professor at Concordia Seminary in St. Louis, whose published essays were described as "doctrinally misleading, subject to much misunderstanding, and a source of unrest within the church." Like Ralph Elliott, his moderate comments on Genesis in particular cast doubt on the literal inerrancy of Scripture, or so said a small but aggressive cabal of ultra-conservatives.

Scharlemann was permitted to read a long statement from the platform and not required to stay for questioning from the floor. He said he was sorry he had caused "unrest in the church," and agreed to withhold four of his papers from further publication, but he retracted nothing.

The debate was long. "No evolution in our schools!" exclaimed the Church's venerable president, John W. Behnken. The anti-Scharlemann spokesmen were the most vociferous; most of the others kept their own counsel—they knew how they were going to vote and what the outcome would be. The doctrinal committee of the Synod brought in its report that "charges of false doctrine have not been sustained to date," and recommended that Scharlemann "be forgiven," whereupon President Behnken urged the delegates to accept the recommendation. "I have been thinking all day," the old man said, "what if Scharlemann should die tonight and I had not forgiven him?"

I sat on a front seat to record the vote—650 for Scharlemann and only 20 against. "What do you think the effect of this will be?" I asked a ranking officer of the Church. He was emphatic and happy in his reply: "We have put that little band of extremists in their place. The convention has served notice that there will be no witch hunts in the Church."

In effect, the delegates had voted to accept an apology that was neither asked nor tendered—to forgive a man for an offense to which he had not pleaded guilty. By a circumlocution worthy of the British Foreign Office in its palmiest days of empire, it managed to save face and to uphold both orthodoxy and academic freedom.

The basis of this action goes back to the same roots that produce an Oswald Hoffmann or a Martin E. Marty. Eight years before the Missouri Synod was founded in 1847, Saxon immigrants established Concordia Seminary in a log cabin in Perry County, Missouri, a few miles from the Mississippi River. Like the Puritan Fathers who founded Harvard, their first concern was to provide for an educated ministry. If it has historically taken a strict view of theology, the Missouri Synod has also been willing to trust the men it trained, once they were given authority. At Cleveland it reaffirmed its respect for learning and its historic obligation to shield its pastors and teachers from persecution by extremists.

Preaching is generally not the Lutheran clergy's strong point. Even in the pulpit, it is the *pastor* who speaks, building up the faithful in a faith in which they have been nurtured from early childhood in parochial school, Sunday school, and communicant classes. A major item at every convention is a doctrinal essay prepared and read by an outstanding Missouri Synod theologian. It is delivered—and listened to—in three or four installments of nearly an hour, a marathon of instruction that would send most non-Lutherans off to the lounge.

In contrast, the Baptist pastor is primarily a preacher and evangelist, always the shepherd in search of lost sheep. Decisions for Christ are not an invention of Billy Graham but standard Southern Baptist practice. A typical convention features a series of stirring evangelistic sermons, fervent gospel preaching without much doctrine and fundamentalist in what doctrine they contain. At one annual session held in St. Louis, three sermons were preached on Sunday, with an even heavier dose of preaching at the pastors' conference on Monday, attended by five thousand ministers from fifty states. They were addressed by L. D. Johnson, professor of Bible at the University of Richmond, who took them to task for stale and irrelevant preaching. Calling for closer attention to the doctrine of Christian nurture, he said, "Too many people really believe that an intelligent, intellectually discriminating person cannot take the gospel seriously, that he has to park his brains in the vestibule when he comes to church."

Johnson speaks for a growing number within his denomination who recognize that the pioneer heritage has its handicaps as well as its glories. Although it has developed many schools and can boast its share of scholars, the Southern Baptist Convention has been slow in according them the kind of respect they command in the Missouri Synod. This reflects a prejudice dating back to covered-wagon days—the distrust of the self-taught and self-reliant for the educational institutions of the patrician Establishment. The setback of the 1962 convention rankles most of all because it is an anachronism as compared, say, with the 1954 convention's response to the Supreme Court decision on school integration. It is by no means the end of the line.

L. D. Johnson also told his audience, "Ministers should ask themselves if they are continuing to be creative in the pulpit or have they been sitting on the same batch of eggs for the last ten or fifteen years, only occasionally changing the location of their nests." As long as there are men like Johnson pointing out the need for change, and ministers ready to heed the challenge, there are grounds for hope of reaching a point where the ouster of a Ralph Elliott would be as unthinkable as that of a Martin Scharlemann.

# 11

# From Apple-Blossom Rhetoric
# to Plain Talk

In the first decade of this century, when the business of the ministry was to preach and no worthy churchman worried about either his inherited way of worshiping God or his country's future, the most mellifluous pulpit voice in the happy land belonged to a Northern Methodist bishop—William A. Quayle (1860–1925). Except for his long black coat, which always needed pressing, and his black string tie—which was more favored by office seekers and undertakers than by the patrician clergy—Bishop Quayle looked like a poet out of a Greenwich Village attic. He never combed his shock of blond hair—I often heard him introduced to congregations as "our beloved Bishop who goes around with his hair apparent."

The milk-and-honey mood of the times and the exalted position of any really articulate preacher encouraged and richly rewarded the Quayle rhetoric, which gushed like a mountain torrent but was as smooth as sliding down banisters. The nation was digesting its first world empire, the fruits of the Spanish-American War—Cuba and the Philippines. The martyred President William McKinley had promised that America would "convert all those heathens." Andrew Carnegie had amassed $350,000,000 to endow higher education and international peace, and to build nearly three thousand public libraries. His

little booklet, *The Gospel of Wealth*, expounded the doctrine
of philanthropy as trusteeship.

In such a bustling but unfinished paradise, glowing with hope
and larceny, the role of church and clergy was to bless the
business of getting on with business, make it respectable, ulcer-
free, and the treasury of Christ's kingdom.

Bishop Quayle was not only a popular preacher; he was a
prolific author of books and articles, and his sermons were as
literary as his essays. One sermon, which I heard twice, began:
"I was lost in thought in my study when a band of estimable
ladies disturbed me to ask that I go into an apple orchard and
bring back an armload of the branches in their pink and white
glory to decorate their church for a festival. Now I am a man
of affairs, but I couldn't find it in my heart to resist a demand
like that. For the beauty of God's world belongs to the beauty
of God's house. And what is so beautiful as an apple tree in
full bloom?"

Today, a congregation would be horrified by the mental picture of a man breaking off branches of an apple tree in bloom,
what with apples a dime apiece at the supermarket.

Quayle was not always sweetness and light. Like nearly all
Methodist preachers of his time, he never hesitated to speak
out on any public question on which he had an opinion or prejudice. In 1916, a national election year, I interviewed him after
he had made a luncheon talk at the Railroad Y.M.C.A. in St.
Louis, and he criticized President Woodrow Wilson for "weakness" in the face of the threat of the German U-boat war on
American shipping. Bishop Quayle was a Northern Methodist
and a Republican, but many of the Southern Methodists in St.
Louis were Democrats, and some of them were furious because
a bishop of a sister church had publicly criticized the Democratic President. The day after my interview appeared in the
old *St. Louis Star*, Bishop Quayle called me and said, "You have
got me drawn and quartered." But he was not too unhappy,
and I have never forgotten his kindness and generosity to a
cub reporter.

One of Bishop Quayle's friends and admirers in his later years was Ivan Lee Holt, who said to me recently, "Bishop Quayle was a truly great preacher and scholar and literary stylist. But he was a poet in his heart and mind, and poets have a difficult time when they must attend to administrative duties. A Methodist bishop must devote a large part of his time doing just that, and the burdens of the office were heavy for a poet like Bishop Quayle."

During the second decade of the century I heard at least fifty imitators of Bishop Quayle, all dreadful. Those ten years covered a world war and its morning-after malaise; we were just in no mood for apple-blossom rhetoric. The tradition endures, however. The last flowery sermon I heard was at the 1961 Southern Baptist Convention in St. Louis. It was delivered by a famous practitioner of the fading art, the venerable Robert G. Lee, who was pastor for many years of the Bellevue Baptist Church in Memphis, Tennessee, and the only man ever to serve two terms as president of the Southern Baptist Convention. Fond of the rounded period, a master of suspense and dramatic illustration, his greatest love is for poetry and he quotes it by the yard. His most famous sermon, "Pay Day Some Day," he has given hundreds of times. It is Jonathan Edwards' "Sinners in the Hands of an Angry God," with love and tenderness added.

Such survivors notwithstanding, the popular style of Protestant preaching took a 180-degree swing during the sixty-five years covered by this book—from apple-blossom rhetoric to plain talk. The new emphasis is on content—the argument—and the pulpit manner is relaxed and conversational in the vernacular. The parson's claw-hammer coat and the deacon's spats went to the attic, or to a Salvation Army retail store. Both the Social Gospel and neo-orthodoxy have been swallowed up by psychological concern and pastoral counseling. About half the sermons I have heard in the past ten years sounded like professional advice for the tired businessman and the new woman floundering in gadgets and leisure.

A serious practitioner of plain talk from the pulpit was Arthur C. Lichtenberger, who recently retired as presiding bishop of the Protestant Episcopal Church.

When Lichtenberger, then dean of Trinity Cathedral in Newark, New Jersey, first came to St. Louis late in 1951 to conduct a preaching mission for men, he had been on the firing line for many years, preaching to cosmopolitan congregations that covered the spectrum of Protestant faith—from left-wing liberalism, politely mixed with unbelief, to rigid orthodoxy. His plain-talk sermons to men were superb. (It is curious that Christian laymen flock to services and sermons reserved for their sex. Perhaps they seek escape from the everyday world which they must share with women, who are less stricken with conformity.)

Lichtenberger's theme was formal, "God Speaks Through You," but his sermon style was shirtsleeves. The burden of his opening address was that though men are sinners and part of a sinful society, there is hope in God's grace. After the sermon, seventy men took part in a discussion period that lasted an hour and a half.

In that mission for men, Lichtenberger was a modern evangelist presenting the claims of Christian faith to a privileged group of men who, he knew, lived and worked and played where they were constantly exposed to every wind that blows from the quarters of skepticism and compromise. He was preaching to free-church men, evangelicals, Episcopalian communicants, and their unbelieving or half-believing friends and neighbors, 120 in all, so he could take nothing for granted, not so much as the simplest statement of doctrine; he had to complete every argument from premise to application. And this was the predicament of the churches and clergy at mid-century: nothing could be taken for granted in religion and morals, not in a generation of secular education and plush aims and antipuritan standards of conduct. The new churches in the high-level suburbs may have most of the money, but they have their grave problems, too.

Lichtenberger returned to St. Louis as its bishop in 1952, a position he held until 1958, when he became presiding bishop of his denomination. For many years he wrote Easter and Christmas messages for the press. These sermonets of about four hundred words received wide circulation. I handled these and other utterances of his for my newspaper and a few religious journals. His literary style is made to order for pulpit delivery and the secular press: short sentences, plain words, vigorous verbs, a minimum of adjectives, brief illustrations, and relevancy to what is on people's minds.

Another American bishop noted for his plain speech is Bishop Gerald Kennedy of the Methodist Church, California area. At the Methodist General Conference at Denver, Colorado, in April 1960, I overheard a discussion among a small group of young ministers in the bookstore. One of them remarked, "I hope we've seen the last Casper Milquetoast book on the ministry." His complaint drew quick response from a colleague: "Read Bishop Kennedy's books—there's the answer to your prayer. Kennedy is tops."

During that very conference, I heard Bishop Kennedy, in a luncheon address heard by more laymen than ministers, demand more frankness, plainer speech, and "literary style" in books on the ministry. He went on to say that the same standards applied to sermons as well as books.

Bishop Kennedy practices what he preached at Denver. Both his books and his sermons have literary style, and they are frank and hard-hitting. He uses the vernacular with greatest ease, and his illustrations are fresh and lively.

The youngest gifted practitioner of plain pulpit talk has resigned his Missouri Synod pulpit in Chicago to give full time—in his case, the understatement of the year—to teaching, editorial duty, and original writing. Martin E. Marty is Associate Professor of Church History at the University of Chicago Divinity School and associate editor of *The Christian Century*. At the age of thirty-six Marty is also a name in radio and television, two other fields in which he has made himself an authority. Men and women of the news media engaged in religious news regard Marty as a genius at the task of the public communication of sixty-four-dollar ideas in five-and-ten-cent words.

Marty's declared purpose, both for the churches and himself, is "to make the Christian faith relevant to persons in the modern world." A master both of vernacular speech and syntax, he is terribly allergic to the formal phrases and pet clichés of the "cowled churchman."

Marty is an exciting figure for religious news editors; they like nothing better than reporting his speeches, which don't have to be translated into everyday speech for the herdsmen on city desks. I heard him address a meeting of clergy and laymen on the public communication of the Christian faith and the good works of the church. It was an exercise in vigor and plain speech. This young man, whose reading of his Lutheran liturgy is a model of decorum, looked more like a college debater: short, tense figure, close-cropped hair, trip-hammer style of delivery (though never dropping his syntax), gesturing like a lightweight boxer with short jabs and uppercuts, but with his belligerent manner belied by an occasional grin and twinkle of eye, reminding his breathless hearers that they were listening to the witty coauthor of *The Christian Century's* "Pen-ultimate." Marty's mastery of change of pace—dropping his machine-gun speech for a brief slow march of words—is charming and effective; I never saw a public speaker who could gauge the responsiveness of his hearers more carefully or more accurately. This facility is especially important for Marty because nine-tenths of the church people who hear him—unless they have heard him before—are unprepared for his plain-talk treatment of august tradition and language. Apparently Marty has read just about everything in his field, and remembers what was grist to his mill. In his talk that afternoon he used at least twenty-five brief illustrations—Scripture verses, quotations from religious and secular sources, even movies. His criticisms of the antique, formal language of church advertising, press releases, convention handouts, public statements, even sermons, was too astringent for the thin skins of some of his hearers, and their questions during the forum after the speech showed that they still clung to the clichés. Marty's witty remarks on religious radio and television programs were devastating. "We must quit using words and phrases in ways that nobody understands any more," he said. "Listen closely to some of the better news broadcasters, see how they bring names and places to life, and remember, their time is limited. We know the people whom we want to reach—we live with them, work with them, listen to their speech every day. Why can't we learn to speak and write their language when we come to spreading word of our churches? Maybe we ought to ask ourselves whether what we have to say is really as important as we think it is. We take its importance for granted, but do the people we want to reach take it for granted? We terribly need self-criticism—to hear what we are saying all the time, by habit, and how it sounds."

Marty is fascinated by the techniques of the news media, movies, and drama, and he is knowledgeable in music and the visual arts. He is a leader and spokesman for the growing number of clergy and other professional workers in the field who are trying to adapt secular arts and techniques for Christian communication.

The Marble Collegiate Church on Fifth Avenue at Twenty-ninth Street, New York, claims to be "the oldest Protestant Church in the United States in continuous service. Founded 1628." Its minister, Norman Vincent Peale, is the most widely known clergyman in the country; churchgoers from many states have told me they always go to hear him when they are in New York. His name is a byword for the religion that works. His best-selling book, *The Power of Positive Thinking*, is a second family Bible in thousands of homes, rich and poor, and is found in more offices than any book in the business category. It has probably been carried more miles in briefcases than any Western paperback. Peale is popular as a preacher, writer, and lecturer, especially among business and professional groups. His lectures are sermons and his sermons lectures, and their sub-

stance is found in all his prolific writings. He makes style and
originality in preaching look ridiculous.

Peale rose to prominence in those hectic years when the national temper was tortured by self-doubt under the impact of
communism, the cold war, and recurring business cycles. He
is a godsend to all those Americans—and they are the majority
—who must see life steadily and see it simple. Peale is a natural
in a society that reads its health in GNP (gross national product) as a physician checks a patient's pulse. Billy Graham takes
sin and repentance too seriously for the general public. Other
preachers find too much fault in the American way of life. A
country that flies "under God" on the masthead is no place for
Jeremiahs. The pursuit of happiness is our religion and Peale
is its prophet.

When I first heard Peale nearly twenty years ago, in St. Louis,
he was, physically, a smaller man than he is today, he spoke
more slowly and with less assurance. But he was already famous
for his books and lectures. I found that he had many friends
among St. Louis business and professional men. When I interviewed Peale, he asked me if I knew his friend William H.
Danforth, who was one of the richest and most prominent business leaders of St. Louis, founder of the Danforth Foundation
and a Congregational layman. He quoted to me Mr. Danforth's
widely circulated creed which I had heard the author recite
several times: "Stand tall, think tall, smile tall, live tall." The
late Mr. Danforth's influence can be traced throughout all of
Peale's writings.

In my interview with him, Peale discussed two problems
facing the churches and clergy in the postwar period: how to
reach and minister to the mobile people in the swollen centers
of population, and how to minister to the lonely, rootless men
and women who had moved to big cities from town and country. As Peale put it, "How can we make the old Gospel real in a
new and strange situation?" Modernizing old church properties
and building new ones was necessary, but this was not the
whole answer, not even the most important part of it, he in-

sisted. "We must re-examine our old ways, including sermons, Sunday schools, youth work, programs for retired persons and the elderly, and our whole program of weekday activities. Our churches must become centers of life where people find help in all their problems.

"But people don't know what their problems are; more often than not they misinterpret them, and here is where faith can help," Peale continued. "This means that ministers and lay people must have imagination. They must be able to see the real needs, the deep needs. I have found that many men and women are unaware of what their real needs are; they are confused. So the churches must enlist the help of experts— physicians and psychiatrists, family welfare workers, personal counselors, professionals in drama and the arts and recreation. Most people have spiritual resources they have never tapped. We must help them discover their own powers, then have the faith to put them to work."

On a Sunday in October 1963, Marble Collegiate Church was filled to the last seat for the second morning service, as it had been at the first. The practical arrangements for handling the coming and going of so many people in an old-fashioned building went off like clockwork—somebody had taken positive thought. No more cosmopolitan congregation was to be found in all New York: hundreds of visitors from everywhere and from all walks of life. Former Vice-President Richard M. Nixon, whose political fortunes in 1960 were not noticeably advanced by Peale's support, sat with his wife and two daughters in a pew near the front.

Worship was not neglected or skimmed through as exercises preliminary to the sermon. It was a surprise to hear an anthem opening the service.

Peale's sermon subject was "Yesterday Ended Last Night," a typical Peale theme and phrase. The sermon was delivered over a microphone in the middle of the wide platform, not from a raised pulpit. The preacher spoke informally in a conversational tone that was pleasant and easily followed. Peale preaches exactly as he writes. Self-assurance is his stock in trade; but very few preachers I have heard came anywhere near his skill in communicating the good feeling to the listener. The sermon held no surprises, the printed topic told the whole story. We cannot live in our yesterdays, only today is real. The sermon structure was letter perfect: brief introduction, fast logical progress, and an eloquent conclusion that joined hope for the weary and disillusioned and remorseful with strict moral accountability. Peale understands as few preachers do the value of suspense and build-up in public speech.

Nobody else could have preached that sermon. In the hands of an amateur, or from an undisciplined mind, it would have been a dismal flop. The textbook sermon has three points; Peale had only one. Out of thirty minutes he gave about ten minutes each to two illustrations taken from his experience with persons who had sought his counsel. Using no notes, quoting his leading characters freely, Peale made two commonplace life stories fascinating. It was wonderful to hear him weave his overlong illustrations into a single thread of meaning. His stories explained themselves and made their meaning perfectly clear. Anyone who has heard Norman Vincent Peale or read his books knows that his mastery of the vernacular is complete. In this sermon he made telephone and sidewalk and household talk sound like quotations from the classics. With most ministers, it is the other way around.

Most of Peale's critics among the clergy exercise themselves in futility. They call him a phony, a peddler of fraudulent patent medicines—the same epithets hurled at Billy Sunday, Mary Baker Eddy, and Billy Graham. They say Peale has no style, no solid content, no depth. And quite naturally they are outraged by his popularity. What they overlook is the secret of his appeal. It is simple: he knows what people are worrying about. He knows because they tell him. Peale sits behind the screen at what is perhaps the most widely attended confessional of any priest or pastor or psychiatrist. His contacts are in person, by mail, and in wide travel. In preaching, he restates these confessions and outpourings of anxiety in words so simple that a child can understand.

The worries and fears and neuroses that provide the framework and half the content of Peale's sermons are common knowledge. They bedevil our table talk, shop talk, and campus talk; our dreams, books, magazines, and the advice columns in newspapers. Peale is a good listener, and he reads with his pen in his hand. He catches more American dialogue than most of our fiction writers. He catches the querulous tone of voice of the man or woman who thinks he has been cheated in the game of life. Job promotions, marriage, the children, love, drinking, sickness, fear of growing old, clinging to the glamour of youth, loneliness, dying. All the terror of life. Where the orthodox minister cites Bible incidents and characters to show that all human problems are recognized there, Peale uses living characters and lets them speak for themselves in the shattered syntax of distress.

His preaching is *ad hoc*. His appeal is to all those people who have lost faith in God, who have nothing to fall back on but themselves, or alcohol, gambling, extramarital sex, pills, and shock treatments. He conducts a glorified clinic in words, the cathedral of plain talk. First there is worship, then there is plain talk about the problems that worship and the memory of worship have failed to solve.

There has been no more radical change in literature, arts, and sciences than in pulpit style over the past fifty years: from Bishop Quayle and Robert G. Lee to Martin Marty and Norman Vincent Peale. Quale and Lee represent the professional elocution of the Chautauqua platform—the solemn periods and grand manner, the elevated thought and vocal tones to match. Marty and Peale are worlds apart in outlook, but both are masters of plain talk—the current idiom familiar from street and table talk, from popular writing, the radio, television, and advertising; homely illustrations; blunt approach to the problems of religion and morals; the masculine tone in delivery; above all, naturalness in everything. The young preacher or layman hear-

ing either of these men for the first time is likely to feel that
there is no art involved and no more effort than in a business
conference at a luncheon table. He couldn't be more wrong. The
plain talk of modern preaching is a difficult art, and there are
few who do it well. It demands disciplined thought and preparation, the utmost care in language, and a trained voice for
enunciation and emphasis—the very highest form of persuasion.

# 12

# Couldn't Hear
# the Neighbors Pray

When in recent years I have heard Negro congregations and
marchers shout and sing "Hallelujah!" the music had a different
bravura from the hymns of victory in which I joined in white
church assemblies forty, fifty, and sixty years ago.

My mind is haunted by the steamy summer night in 1941—
corn- and cotton-growing weather—in a housing community for
Negro farm laborers and unemployed established and maintained by the Farm Security Administration, in which I was
then employed. The children of the camp presented a program
of music and readings for the approval of their white neighbors
and townspeople. The boys and girls were all scrubbed up and
neatly dressed in their Sunday best. Their faces and eyes and
hair and bodies plainly showed the salutary effects of the first
adequate diets they and their parents had ever enjoyed—government sponsored of course—cod liver oil and orange juice,
supervised play, medical, dental, and nursing care, and decent
housing with window screens in place of miserable shacks. The
Negro women in that tight little community were good house-
keepers and food canners, and attractive personalities, too.

The long program in the community house that night closed
with those children singing "Sweet land of liberty, Of thee I

sing." The master of ceremonies was their unsalaried preacher, Brother Mac.

To me, Brother Mac is a symbol of the miracle of the Negro revolution that saved our time in the Christian experience of grace from futility by the wind of adversity. By the children of adversity. What makes the story wonderful is that Negro Christians organized the revolution and launched it with sermons, hymn singing, and prayers from their poverty-stricken churches in the ghettos where the white Christians had held them prisoner for centuries. Many of their churches were bombed or burned by night riders and white mobs.

I first met Brother Mac at the county welfare office where he had gone to intercede for a few of his church families who had been dropped from the relief rolls. I was there in behalf of a white woman who, with her nine children, had been deserted by the husband and father.

Brother Mac would have been distinguished in any gathering, white or black. He was a handsome old man, large, erect, with graying stubble on his face and a deep bass voice. He was neatly dressed and his arms and shoulders under his blue shirt were thick and powerful. He had been a sharecropper on the same big farm for nearly thirty years when the 1938 farm control law made it more profitable for the landowner to terminate the traditional sharecropping arrangement and hire only day laborers. Brother Mac was now living in the FSA camp and supporting himself and his wife by seasonal work on nearby farms. They had a hard row to hoe, for farm wages were low and the hired hand suffered weeks of idleness every year.

I was fascinated and shamed by Brother Mac's courtly manner and dignity in answering the unfriendly questions of the young woman welfare worker—her prejudiced attitude was as belligerent as she could make it. I have never forgotten the unhappy expression on Brother Mac's face when he was turned away. I was treated with utmost respect, and the welfare worker assured me that my client would be taken care of.

On a Sunday not long after this encounter, a Negro was

lynched in Sikeston, Missouri, where I lived and where my
office was. He had been accused of killing a white man. Sikeston
was a churchgoing community, and the small white mob picked
the hour before Sunday noon for the deed; most of the citizens
would be in church and there wouldn't be many on the downtown streets. The mob broke into the old jail with the greatest
of ease, dragged the Negro from his cell, shot him to death,
soaked him with gasoline, and burned him. They tied his body
to the rear fender of a car and dragged it slowly through the
Negro district across town from the jail. My three teenage
children at home, who had been in Sunday school and church,
were in a panic of fear. But in the community, the incident
of the lynching was passed over, liquidated, as if it had been
no more deplorable than the accidental shooting of a farmer's
cow by a dove hunter. Nobody was arrested, nobody punished,
though members of the unmasked mob were recognized by
the police.

It was one day that week that I went to visit Brother Mac at
his little unpainted plank-on-end church in a clearing in the
cotton fields. Brother Mac and I sat on the long, low, narrow
front porch of his church for our talk, the black gold of the
white man's land under our feet. The Negro preacher had never
walked anywhere in his native land except with the white man's
permission. About half a dozen men from his congregation
joined us, but not one of them spoke a word all evening; they
listened to us. My host used perfect English; he had graduated
from high school and worked his way through two years at
a Negro college in Mississippi. He moved North after his planta-
tion-riding boss accused him of stirring up trouble among the
field hands—he was called an "uppity nigger" because he spoke
good English.

I asked Brother Mac how he could hold his temper and
dignity under such abuse as he received at the welfare office.
"When two fools meet, there is trouble," he said. "But when
a wise man meets a fool there is no trouble; the wise man
walks away."

That was the Negro strategy of nonresistance by which he had lived at least sixty years—I knew he had grandchildren in college. Martin Luther King, Jr., did not have to import the revolutionary method of nonviolence from India's Gandhi; his own people, even he himself, had followed it from time unremembered as the first law of nature—self-preservation. They had committed it to heart first at home, then in Sunday school and church and in the rotten shacks where they received "separate but equal" education. The method of survival belonged in the same silent arsenal as the wisdom to get off the sidewalk to let the white man pass. So Brother Mac was giving me his Christian witness in an alien, hostile society that exploited his labor while it held him in poverty under the restraint of fear for his life. Now it is hard for the white minister to enter that underground world of his Negro brother, for he hasn't had to live and preach in fear of his life—unless he was a Yankee stirring up trouble among the "happy darkies" in Mississippi. As a little boy in that state Brother Mac had shared the terror in his parents' house and eyes at a lynching.

In our conversation, I made several openings for him to bring up the lynching in Sikeston of the previous Sunday. No comment. I tried but failed again to lead him to talk about himself and his people and their trials and hopes. He wanted only to talk about the Bible and Christian faith. He quoted many passages in his beautiful deep voice; the Psalms and the Beatitudes were his favorites.

The next Sunday I found his little frame church filled with worshiping families on the beastly hot day in July—the women used small paper fans which advertised an undertaker's establishment in town. I was greeted politely. Brother Mac appeared in a black suit, starched white shirt, and black string tie. Except for the color of his skin he reminded me of bishops and circuit riders I had heard in my youth. His sermon was on the miracle of the Red Sea crossing, Exodus 14:21–22: "And Moses stretched out his hand over the sea; and the Lord caused the sea to go back by a strong east wind all that night, and made

the sea dry land, and the waters were divided. And the children
of Israel went into the midst of the sea upon the dry ground:
and the waters were a wall unto them on their right hand, and
on their left." It was a sermon of eloquence and color and
dramatics—the sounds of the wind and the water and the
Israelites' bare feet. The preacher was interrupted many times
by low cries from his congregation: "How true! How true!"

A young woman in a white dress and big white hat, a school-
teacher, played the reed organ well, and we sang several familiar hymns. But the one I remember best was new to me then:

> We shall not be moved.
> Like a tree planted by the waters,
> We shall not be moved.

Not long afterward I was invited to speak at a Sunday-afternoon meeting of another Negro church. The congregation,
much poorer than Brother Mac's group, met in a roofed but
unwalled tabernacle with wooden benches in a makeshift camp
for dispossessed sharecroppers near Poplar Bluff, Missouri. The
camp's existence was a thorn in the side of the white farming
community. Established by the Negroes themselves, it received
aid from the Farm Security Administration and from white
friends in St. Louis. Local politicians told me that the isolated
Negro settlement with makeshift buildings concealed a Communist cell.

The camp's pastor and manager was Owen Whitfield, an
organizer of the Southern Tenant Farmers' Union. He was
the leader of a demonstration in southeast Missouri in which the
families of dispossessed Negro sharecroppers camped along the
highway—to the dismay and fear of the white power structure.
Whitfield led a fiery service of worship which was more a
community sing, with frequent exhortations by the leader. This
congregation also sang the hymn "We Shall Not Be Moved."
They added a stanza in tribute to Whitfield—"He shall not be
moved." In recent years, a similar song has come to the fore
of the civil rights movement—"We Shall Overcome."

I talked to that congregation about the various programs of the Farm Security Administration. Never in my life have I encountered such skepticism. Whitfield was cordial, but his people were not. The atmosphere was hostile to all whites, including me. I should have been better prepared for an awkward, embarrassing occasion, for my experience with racial separation in the churches was lifelong.

I was a member of the white congregation that built an imposing white stone church in midtown St. Louis in 1908. I remember the Sunday when, with the galleries filled and standees everywhere, we dedicated our beautiful new sanctuary. Two years later we sold our church to the Negro congregation that occupies it today. My old congregation has moved three times to keep a jump ahead of the Negro tide. What we harassed white Christians needed but the Lord failed to provide was another miracle of the Red Sea crossing. The Negro congregation in my old church is several times larger than the fleeing body of whites.

My old church was again packed to the galleries when I revisited it; men were standing at the rear and along the walls. It was a well-dressed, middle-class congregation including many professional men, businessmen, and schoolteachers. They were almost gay in spirit, more cheerful people than I was used to in church. The singing by three large choirs—a hundred children in white and black gowns sang from the gallery—with organ and piano accompaniment, was thrilling; the people heartily sang the Gloria and Doxology as well as several hymns. The service lasted two hours and included three offerings.

The pastor, William Cooper, now retired, lived in the two-and-a-half-story brick and stone Victorian parsonage on the church grounds. It had high ceilings and ornate woodwork, a hand-carved black walnut staircase with a stained glass window at the landing; tall, slender windows with marble sills on the first floor, parquet floors in the large living room and dining room. The minister's wife was a collector of antiques—the crystal chandelier over the long dining table would have brought more at auction than all my first-floor furnishings. The walls of the hallway, living room, and dining room were hung with the minister's paintings, most of them portraits of Negro models chosen to portray the very wide variety of racial characteristics. Cooper has published several books including a volume of sermons.

This big, hearty man who loves elegant living and has pursued it all his adult life is a conservative in all things. "My mother was born a slave in South Carolina," he told me. "When I knew her she was a stylish lady. I thank my God every day for blessing me with a good life as a citizen of the greatest country on earth. I have traveled over the land for forty years and have been in an ideal position to see the improvement in the climate of race relations. The two races must march forward together; in a democracy like ours, neither race can profit at the expense of the other. The unhappy events of the past few years have not shaken my faith. Violence defeats itself."

William Cooper is middle-class American from head to toe. He is as ruggedly individualistic in philosophy as a Vermont farmer. He fought valiantly for his own people when they were being exploited and cheated by chiseling white tradesmen, landlords, politicians, and professional men. He delivered many of his church families from the toils of the loan sharks. At the same time, he has held an honored place in the interchurch activities of his community. But he did this as an individual minister. His people had no part in it. His large congregation has remained within the separate Negro Christian community.

And I grew up in my white world under an article of faith: "All Negroes and poor whites are alike!"

A recent conversation with a Negro minister reminded me of what many church leaders—not pastors, but officers of interchurch councils and denominations—fail to see: the enormous roadblocks still in the way of natural, cordial, fruitful race relations in religion. This minister has a very large middle- and upper-middle-class congregation with one of the most beautiful churches in St. Louis. He holds a doctorate in theology from a leading Eastern seminary. He is an outstanding leader in the upper class of the Negro community. He is a man of courage and pride. Most of all, he is a gentleman. Even when his resentment of injustices and rationalizations is blazing, his manner is still superior.

"Why have you quit going to meetings of the interracial, interdenominational ministerial alliance?" I asked. "I'm sick and tired of listening to all their talk about brotherhood," he replied. "Why don't they practice what they preach? When the white ministers and their churches are willing to accept us as brothers I'm ready to join them."

A Southern-born white minister accepted a call to a large church in a Northern city after giving his promise never to mention the race problem. Here is what he told me after the schools and a few churches in his city had integrated: "You have no idea of the ordeal I'm going through. It took me ten years to reach the place where I could work freely and happily with Negro ministers and lay people in our church federation, my national church convention, and in the National Council of Churches. I know that segregation is on the way out. But I really think my own church would rather die than accept a Negro member."

One Monday about twelve years ago I took part in the annual meeting of a regional labor council that embraced a large number of unions. The meeting was held in the ballroom of a downtown hotel with some three hundred men and women attending. The hotel management had at first refused to promise to serve luncheon to the Negro delegates, but under considerable pressure from the labor council it relented. There were no incidents, and everybody was happy.

The very same evening I covered a dinner meeting at one of the oldest and largest churches in the city. There were two hundred guests. The only Negro to be seen was wearing a white linen jacket, and the minister and church members called him "George." Today that church is still segregated in a neighborhood that has become Negro in population.

I was invited to give a talk on my experiences as a religion editor before the very large women's organization of a historic church. When I arrived at the beautiful old church, the chairman of the meeting took me aside to explain, "Now, remember, we just don't talk about the Negro problem in this church." I could see Negro children playing in yards across the street. The most prominent layman of that church recently repeated his standing threat to his pastor: "The first time I see a Negro walking down our aisle, that is when I get up and walk out." The layman is a national officer of his liberal denomination. The congregation, which celebrated its centennial many years ago, is dying on the white vine. Two different Negro congregations have made liberal offers to purchase the expensive property.

The Negro drive for long-denied rights has been a two-edged sword. It has opened up for all the world to see the established dual structure of American church life, and at the same time it has sharpened the long-standing divisions within the dominant group. The clergy is divided over the issue, but then the clergy was always divided over issues that are current. Congregations are shown up as lagging behind the clergy on a moral issue which the state snatched from the church. A majority of the clergy lags behind their denominational leaders, and the denominational administrations, with very few exceptions, trail the National Council of Churches.

For example, President Ben M. Herbster, of the United Church of Christ, has given vigorous leadership in the drive for integration from top to bottom. With some difficulty he obtained the support of the 1963 General Synod of his church. But it quickly became clear that many older officers of national boards and commissions were cool and reluctant, while many pastors and a very large segment of the church membership were unhappy and hostile. (I have listened to them and read their correspondence.) A powerful figure in this denomination's movement toward integration is Truman B. Douglass, executive vice-president of the United Church Board for Homeland Ministries, who has laid the issue on the line in forceful preaching and writing, by quiet efforts to persuade businessmen to implement the church's resolution in employment and pay, and by efforts to get his church to withdraw its investments from business firms that retain segregation.

Other denominations engaged in the Johnny-come-lately crusade are having about the same experience. Methodists, Presbyterians, Baptists, Disciples, and Lutherans are all deeply divided over the issue. Roman Catholic cardinals, archbishops, and bishops have had to deal with recalcitrant clergy and parishioners. Leaders of the national communions realize that the bulk of the opposition to integration has gone underground except in the Deep South; it is present everywhere, but sullenly silent. "It is easier," said a home missions secretary, "to get a ringing declaration from our national convention than to persuade a local congregation to accept a Negro family for membership."

A New York Negro attorney told a Lutheran national convention, "Local churches tend to be more like social clubs than churches." In dealing with racial problems their members show "the middle-class outlook and behavior patterns."

This is all too true, yet things are changing. Among the estimated 250,000 people who took part in the historic March on Washington on August 28, 1963, as many as one-third were white—this included many whole congregations. Thousands of them rode in buses, trains, cars, and trucks all night, many of them two or three days. And a year later the Civil Rights Act was passed. When Senator Richard Russell of Georgia, leader of the filibuster against enactment of the law, was asked what groups were most responsible for the overwhelming vote in favor of it, he named first the churches and clergy.

The leader and spokesman of the clergy in the March on Washington was from Georgia too—Martin Luther King, Jr., copastor of Ebenezer Baptist Church in Atlanta. His voice thrilled the massed marchers and the television and radio listeners as he spoke of his "Dream" of his country delivered from strife and bitterness and united as brothers, good neighbors, and friends. But King was more than a leader, spokesman, and organizer; he was a symbol of the better angels of his fellow citizens' natures.

I first heard Martin Luther King preach in 1956, when the Montgomery bus boycott was under way. He came to St. Louis to deliver a series of five sermons. His deep voice resounded in the downtown Episcopal cathedral, enunciating a great passage from First Corinthians: "But God hath chosen the foolish things of the world to confound the wise." This young minister was on his way, with detours in jails, to first place among the Christian clergy of America and the world. Eight years later he was awarded the Nobel Peace Prize.

But more newsworthy than his sermons was King's session with the ministerial alliance. The organization of Protestant pastors has always been interracial. But this did not mean that all the white ministers who listened to King and asked him questions that Monday agreed with the aims and methods of his revolution. He had stalwart friends and supporters in the luncheon crowd, but aside from the Negro pastors, they were a minority. King was a model of poise and patience; he never raised his voice. He wasn't trying to preach a second sermon to the preachers; he talked informally and quietly about the race tensions in both South and North, of what he and his group were doing to improve the situation, and what all churches and clergy could do to help.

King's encounter with the Protestant clergy was a revelation of the equivocal position of the churches and white ministers on an issue that since has jelled. My estimate on the occasion was that most of the white ministers were unresponsive to his appeal. There were others who sympathized with King but who felt that their own people were "not ready for integration."

On another occasion, King was the only Negro present at a small luncheon. From the moment he was introduced around the table, he was quite at ease, though most of the guests were total strangers. His manner was completely relaxed, warm, and friendly. As a professional journalist who had been interviewing celebrities for forty years, I felt that I was examining a new type of spiritual, moral, and political leader. He believed deeply in the nonviolent power of love, and he was a Negro born to live in equality and fraternity with men of all races.

King is not only a spellbinder who has mastered the modern arts of communication; he is a devout believer and loyal churchman, the product of evangelical faith. At the time when rival leaders of the movement scorned "white man's religion," King keeps that faith. Though righteously impatient for long-overdue social change, he has kept the emotional energy of the Negro revolution wired to religious faith and to church life, insisting that his followers respond to racism with dignity and forbearance, substituting love for vengeance. He has always welcomed and acknowledged support from whites and remained close enough to see their troubled consciences and to forgive shortcomings. Despite the whole sorry history of persecution, he chose to set an example rather than mount a vicious tirade, and his example has spurred both Negroes and whites to action.

The Negro has never totally lacked white support, from Elijah Lovejoy, the abolitionist editor murdered by a white mob at Alton, Illinois, in 1837, to Bruce Klunder, who died during a civil rights protest in Cleveland, Ohio, in 1964. Both men were Presbyterian ministers. Other examples could be cited, many of them far less dramatic. Even in the worst times, there have been at least a few men who spoke out, whatever the consequences, and in recent days the churches have been deluged with applications to serve in the Mississippi Summer Project and other such ventures in brotherhood, both North and South.

Even in the local churches the walls of segregation are slowly crumbling. Biracial staffs are less a rarity than formerly, and this is even truer at the level of denominational boards and agencies. Yet the biggest problem lies ahead—bringing the races together in one community of mutual respect, forbearance, and love, making the idea of Brotherhood Sunday an unnoticed, everyday experience. The full solution to this problem can come only from a widespread change of heart, the conversion of local congregations and clergy. Interracial ministerial associations, choirs, and the like are only steps along the way, means consistent with the end, which is a miracle of grace.

I have visited many churches where this miracle has taken place. Usually the little children are the first to achieve the fun of fraternity, unruffled by one another's color. They are born that way. Adults of both races have much to unlearn. We have the laws. We have church resolutions, too. And we have the example, first of all in Jesus himself, but also in pragmatic American, down-to-earth terms. All we need now is the will, the courage to change.

# 13

# All Headed
# for the Same Place

"Preachers love to ride horses," a denominational officer said recently. "If they find a horse that looks good to them, they'll ride it to death. This is what happened to church union. Most of the preaching about it was wishful thinking."

He was talking about the Blake-Pike proposal that set off a blaze of enthusiasm in December 1960 and resulted in more sermons, resolutions, and public statements than any event since Martin Luther nailed his theses to the door. Its ramifications provided me with more news stories than anything else in my career as a religion editor.

There have been important strides, the greatest of which was the founding of the National Council of Churches in 1945. Considering the Balkanized structure of Protestantism, it is a miracle that forty-one denominations with some 40,000,000 members are thus brought together. For all its limitations, the National Council surpasses any previous body except the Roman Catholic Church in size, extent of organization, and variety of services.

However symbolic of cooperation and unity it is, nevertheless the National Council is by common consent only an agency of its autonomous member churches. Liberals may favor strengthening its authority, but they are outnumbered by denominational conservatives who fear that it might become a "super-church."

There have been mergers in this century, but nearly all have followed denominational lines, bringing together separate Methodist bodies to form the present Methodist Church, bringing together Lutherans within the American Lutheran Church, or Presbyterians within the United Presbyterian Church. The exceptions are few, the most notable being that between Congregationalists and the Evangelical and Reformed Church of German ancestry, which formed the United Church of Christ.

The Blake-Pike proposal would have effected mergers on a grand scale across denominational lines, joining together Presbyterians, Episcopalians, Disciples, the United Church, and other bodies into a huge new Protestant organization. Had this occurred, it would have been big news indeed. After more than five years, the proposal is still being discussed, in periodic consultations and in commissions assigned to "further study of areas of differences and agreement." But the blaze of enthusiasm dwindled to a flicker by the end of 1962, and not a single merger came out of all the furor. By then, all eyes were on the Vatican Council—the torch had passed to Pope John and Cardinal Bea.

"Maybe the experience was good for all of us," the denominational leader added. "It sent us back to tend our own gardens, which sure are full of weeds. It was just too bad for all those fired-up crusaders who broke their lances and fell off their horses. Next time, they may be more realistic. Christian unity will come in God's time, and the road ahead is long and rocky." How this second miracle of unity will come no doubt will surprise liberals and conservatives alike. The dream of one universal church is as old as Jesus' prayer in the Fourth Gospel, "that they all may be one."

When the army of news-media men and women reached Cleveland, Ohio, on November 27, 1950, for the Constituting Convention of the new National Council of Churches, the city was almost paralyzed by a blizzard. There were no streetcars, no buses, and private automobiles were forbidden to appear downtown. A man-made mountain of snow and ice on the plaza in front of our hotel reached to the third floor. And the auditorium was a mile away on the lake front, where the wind blew hardest and coldest. The newsmen pooled taxicabs, and police looked the other way when we packed the cab like college boys in a telephone booth.

Although the storm delayed the arrival of many delegates, the convention opened on time, moved like greased lightning, accomplished what it had come to do, and there was no end of good news stories to file. The host and unofficial travel guide and factotum of the newspaper crowd was the late Frank Stewart, religion editor of the *Cleveland Press* for many years, and founder and first president of the national Religious Newswriters' Association. On the first evening, Stewart said of the delegates, "These boys and girls know why they are here, and no nonsense. We're going to watch a convention run like clockwork."

The hotel lobbies and coffee shops swarmed with delegates who were seeking shelter from the cold outside and sharing the preconvention gossip of anticipation and foretelling that generally is more enjoyable than the formal proceedings themselves. There was apprehension, too.

A few officers of the very large and energetic United Church Women, which was to become a department of the new council, told me they were afraid that the enormous, male-run organization might cramp the women's style—try to censor outspoken public statements on the liberal side of controversial issues. This has not happened, at least so far as the public news of United Church Women has disclosed.

Work on the structure of the new council had been in progress for several years. A key task was to dispel the notion that the organization would be nothing more than the successor to the Federal Council of Churches. The old council was torn by dissension and badgered by political witch-hunters and fundamentalist church groups.

The National Council united within its framework twelve different interdenominational agencies—the Federal Council was liquidated. These member groups included the Foreign Missions Conference, which had been in existence since 1893; the Missionary Education Movement; the Home Mission Council of North America; the International Council of Religious Education; Church World Service; United Churchmen; and the Church Women.

The official organizational chart, which newsmen found to be bewildering when they had to write their stories, showed ninety-four different departments, boards, bureaus, commissions, and committees. (The fantastic structure of the National Council has been overhauled since 1962, but it is still a tribute to the statistical mind.)

One of the most significant acts of the Constituting Convention was to name Henry Knox Sherrill the first president—the term is three years. He was presiding bishop of the Protestant Episcopal Church. The press room knew that nobody else was under consideration. The election of Sherrill was a brilliant stroke; it got the new council off on the right foot. His first press conference, however, was a disappointment, for he was very reticent. Bishop Sherrill was chosen as a gesture toward Protestant unity. The Constituting Convention knew that the National Council must not start life as a public-affairs forum or debating society; it had to be the dignified agency of churches and churchmen, the very groups whose bad dream was to lose their denominational identity. And Bishop Sherrill, who has always been a liberal, was above everything else a staunch churchman, a priest of the church. He was rector of the Church of Our Saviour in Brookline, Massachusetts, from 1920 to 1922; rector of Trinity Church, Boston (the church of Phillips Brooks) from 1923 till his election as bishop of Massachusetts in 1930, and presiding bishop from 1947 till his retirement in 1958. He has long been identified with interchurch affairs, and he has served as a president of the World Council of Churches.

Bishop Sherrill's term as president of the National Council of Churches was a honeymoon compared to most of the years of the old Federal Council, and many years since for the National Council.

Ten years later, on December 4, 1960, three thousand delegates, alternates, consultants, and staff members, and five thousand visitors, were gathered in Catholic San Francisco for the opening of the triennial General Assembly of the National Council of Churches. The organization was about to wind up its three stormiest years, during which it had been under constant and well-financed attacks from the political right and fundamentalist religionists—the race issue was heating up. The Council had rallied to the courageous leadership of an outspoken liberal clergyman, Edwin T. Dahlberg. In the crowded press room it was a well-kept secret that the next president would be a multimillionaire layman who would be expected to draw off some of the heat from the Babbitts and Pews and McCarthys among the Council's member denominations. Irwin J. Miller made his friends happy and confounded his potential enemies by proving to be another stalwart liberal, a friend of organized labor, opposed to the right-to-work law of his own state of Indiana, the most conservative state in politics and religion north of the Mason-Dixon line.

The news-media men and women at San Francisco gave as much space and time to Miller as to the convention. A manufacturer of Diesel engines and a banker like his grandfather, his personal estate was estimated by *Fortune* magazine at sixty million dollars. He was then the angel of *The Christian Century* and is a member of the Christian Church (Disciples), as is President Lyndon B. Johnson. Miller has long been active in the movement for church unity, but gets precious little support on his home ground.

Immediately after his election, Miller held his first news conference, a National Council ritual. When he came into the press room, the news corps was astonished to see an industrial tycoon who looked and talked like a professor of classics in a

Tidewater college. Miller was shy, soft-spoken, unsmiling; his interviewers had grown used to the approachability and friendliness of his predecessor, Edwin Dahlberg of the powerful voice and hearty laughter, whose good stories and counterthrusts had enlivened many a press conference during his three-year term. Dahlberg had quickly learned the first names of the reporters and never forgot them.

But when the new president started answering questions, he was quick, concise, and forthright; he dodged no question or issue. "I will now have to spend a good deal of time in the New York offices of the National Council," Miller said, "but I'm already acquainted with the over-all organization and programs, and I shall give them my full support. I believe in what the Council is doing, and I intend to follow the general policies that have succeeded so well under my distinguished predecessors. The National Council has established itself as an important, valuable agency and spokesman of the churches; I hope to see its support greatly increase."

Miller made it plain that he would not back down before the vociferous criticism of the Council for "meddling in politics." He said he had long supported church unity and would "continue to support the movement."

The news hounds filed stories they were happy to write—whether their editors were or not—stories they had not expected to get. In forty minutes, the gentle-mannered multimillionaire from Indiana had made friends of the press crew, even of the few who didn't agree with his liberal views.

Miller is a "natural" for the feature writers in the press room. He lives in a French chateau in Columbus, Indiana, collects modern art, reads his New Testament in Greek, and plays Bach on his violin. He is a tall, handsome Oxford scholar with a scholar's stoop and a prodigious memory for the Greek and Latin classics.

This scholarly millionaire loves to preach from New Testament texts. In his three years of travel and preaching from coast to coast, Miller demanded the same freedom, which he

himself had earned and could safely indulge, for small fry
who were bound to get hurt unless well-placed churchmen
stood up to be counted. His money and his Greek and Latin
made him an awkward target for his critics. This amazing new
president further demanded freedom for the National Council
of Churches to continue making liberal pronouncements in the
controversial areas of politics and society, especially on civil
rights and human welfare. He stoutly supported the movement
for church unity among the Council's member churches.

At San Francisco more than a hundred men and women from
the press, radio, television, and church papers needled one
another over free coffee and doughnuts (their fare in public)
for prognostications of a newsworthy if not history-making
General Assembly. We were also on advance notice of pre-
assembly fireworks. One ghost of Protestant politics had been
laid: a national election exactly one month before had established that a Roman Catholic can be elected President of the
United States.

The launching of the Blake-Pike proposal for Protestant unity
could not have been better staged by Joshua Logan. The stage
itself could not have been wider, the audience more inclusive.
The National Council had brought together representatives of
all the Protestant and Orthodox communions that had any
concern for church unity and could be persuaded to talk about
it seriously. Eugene Carson Blake was a past president of the
Council and top executive officer of one of its largest member
churches—Stated Clerk of the United Presbyterian Church,
U.S.A. He was an ordained minister, a scholar, an effective
administrator, and he was popular with the rank and file of the
National Council's numerous staff, and also the press.

It was known, of course, that Blake was to preach the sermon
at eleven o'clock at Grace Episcopal Cathedral and that Bishop
James A. Pike would be in his bishop's chair. What was not
announced was that immediately following the sermon, Bishop
Pike would give his blessing to the proposal for union.

It was the gossip in the hotel lobbies and coffee shops that

Blake would put forward a dramatic proposal calling for action. (I had been put on notice at my desk in St. Louis three weeks in advance.) There were no advance copies of the sermon—both Blake and Pike were already distinguished for their sense of timing as well as for their courage. They realized that their proposal for action on what everybody was talking about must be a package deal, and it must pre-empt the General Assembly floor before it got under way on its own track. One more piddling suggestion would be a dud; it would land in the graveyard of pious hopes jealously tended by the denominational top brass. Nobody in the religious arena knew better than Blake and Pike how to circumvent this fate: they used the element of surprise and the mass media to bypass entrenched ecclesiastical interests and catch the eye and mind of local congregations and clergy. Yet even those two valiant churchmen must have been surprised by the extent of national news coverage.

The Blake-Pike proposal is in deep trouble today; that is, it has fallen into the numb hands of duly elected commissions whose love of meetings is as passionate as their devotion to self-preservation. Nevertheless the bold plan achieved its initial success instantly—it put Protestantism in general and denominational bureaucrats in particular on the defensive in the universal struggle for peace and harmony in the Christian world. And who would have thought in December 1960 that the principal ally of a Presbyterian stated clerk and an Episcopal bishop was going to be an aged pope in Rome?

The details of the Blake-Pike proposal are as familiar as the ringing of church bells; they quickly became part of our Sunday talk. Blake's sermon covered the waterfront by calling for a united church that would be "truly Catholic, truly Evangelical, and truly Reformed." Nobody could object to that. Nobody was left out. Spelling out his grand scheme, Blake proposed that a start be made by bringing together in one Protestant body of over twenty million members his own church, Pike's church, the Methodist Church, and the United Church of Christ, itself a recent merger. Other denominations would also be invited to join this massive Protestant union.

Within five minutes after the benediction at Grace Cathedral I heard in the assembly press room the first criticism and gainsaying from clergy and laymen of the four denominations involved, including Methodist bishops on both sides of the fence. The sermon received many times the amount of publicity and pro and con discussion as all the proceedings of the National Council of Churches which convened the same evening. By eight o'clock the following morning the press room was filled to the point of nuisance by groups engaged in debate. Blake and Pike were among the first to arrive. I talked to both of them. They were in high spirits over the response they had met, but they agreed that their proposal faced a long, hard fight.

A veteran churchman serving church relations remarked, "American Protestantism hasn't been so deeply stirred by a sermon since Emerson's Divinity School Address in 1838." It really was a masterpiece. It covered the background of need, the anticipated objections, the hopes which inspired the plan, and steps to be taken, one by one, toward the goal. Its mixed reception and its stubborn survival are proof that the spoken word can be a powerful weapon, especially when it deals in plain speech with an issue which other speakers befog with piety and fancy rhetoric.

As an example of preaching, the Blake sermon was a happy blend of pulpit and pew—exalted in sentiment, practical in conclusions. Its distinguished team of collaborators are much closer to lay opinion than the rank and file clergy. This is not to be wondered at, for both men serve communions in which laymen (though not women) play a strong, sometimes controlling hand in policies and programs at all levels of church life. The two denominations are working closely and happily together at many places after so many years of separateness. In our general society their people are as much alike as two peas in a pod. Presbyterians are rapidly becoming city-minded, as Episcopalians have always been.

It has not been many years since Pike was himself a layman; first Roman Catholic, then an unattached unbeliever, then an Episcopal layman studying for the priesthood. In recent years his sermons and addresses and books show that he has never lost touch with the lay mind, including its growing impatience with denominational machinery and stained-glass mentality. Bishop Pike shocks and irritates more clergy than laymen. He has always been able to take a good long look at Protestantism from the outside.

As for Eugene Blake, he of course knows what is in the minds of laymen, for as executive officer of his denomination he is in daily touch with more laymen than ministers. He is an executive, not a pastor. Besides, he is a sophisticated man like his friend Pike. Both men are familiar with the successful projects on which their two communions are working together.

Blake and Pike work well together, too, for they complement each other—as the oldtimers from the press corps remarked after the two churchmen had performed as a team in launching their ambitious proposal for church union. Blake is a big, hearty man, who played football at Princeton University in 1927 and 1928. To newsmen who covered the National Council when Blake was president, he was known then and now as the "Presbyterian Pope," and the reporters still carry a torch for him.

Bishop Pike is an intense individual and, for all his liberal views, very episcopal in bearing. He is the scholarly type, and generally gives the impression of a busy man who at the moment is deeply engaged in profound thought. In football, Blake would carry the ball; Pike would call signals from the bench.

The General Assembly of the National Council was a made-to-order sounding board, but nothing could be done about Blake's proposal there—he was bypassing the Council. He also knew that if and when Protestant unity comes to pass it will not be in solemn assemblies; they cannot even share holy communion, having taken out their various patents on the bread and wine. Not from prolonged expense-account negotiations over *trivia*—the ritual of the laying on of hands, the wearing of clerical collars, and how much water is required to drown the old Adam. Not even by taking referendums.

The Blake-Pike thunderbolt accomplished a most salutary thing: it called the bluff of all pious pleaders who are prepared to talk their lives out about "all the things we have in common" but are unwilling to take the first practical step toward union of their churches. A bill of particulars was laid before the whole Christian world by managed newsmaking; specifically, the twenty million members of the four churches involved know what was proposed for them so they may follow the top-level negotiations.

Pope John XXIII's call for the Vatican Council in 1961 took the whole world by surprise—not only the faithful and the "separated brethren" but the College of Cardinals and the Roman Curia itself. Members of the Religious Newswriters Association voted this the top news story of the year.

Protestantism, when it had recovered from the shock of taking second place in church news, responded in expected ways. Churches and clergymen affiliated with the World Council of Churches responded with massive good will, prayer, and speculation. Sermons on Christian unity took a new line—all roads led to Rome. The fundamentalists recoiled, then accused the World Council of standing with hat in hand at St. Peter's gate prepared to sacrifice Reformation faith for a mess of statistical pottage. Some of them denounced the whole business as an Anglican-Roman plot. American newspapers and magazines, secular and religious, printed millions of words on the first ecumenical council of the Roman Catholic Church to be called in a century; the topic was fascinating not only because it was unexpected but also for its element of mystery—everybody wanted to know what Pope John had in mind and what would be the results.

What about the man in the street? He was interviewed on news microphones from coast to coast. His response to the news from Rome was a beautiful thing—churchmen will have something to answer for at the bar of judgment if they betray or circumvent the common man's dream of unity and peace. At my church news desk, and over my telephone there and at home, I had talks every day with Catholics, Protestants, and unbelievers about the prospects for Christian unity. On buses and on the street one heard the discussions and arguments. My Catholic neighbors and friends talked more to me about their church and religion in a year than they had done in twenty years. Catholic lay persons were eager to find what was the reaction to the news from Rome among non-Catholics. It was another era of good feeling for which Americans had long been waiting.

In this country the cause of unity was ill served by the over-enthusiasm of some of the Protestant observers at the Second Vatican Council. I read reams of their reports and listened to others. Much of it was half-baked. Sometimes the novelty of the surprise experience, the pageantry, the presence of so many notable personages—perhaps also the promptings of a fresh hope—overwhelmed a reporter's nose for news. History was forgotten in the magnificence of a scene where new history was to be made. One bishop observer, in an hour and a half address after returning from Rome, left the general impression with twelve hundred Protestant listeners that Protestant-Catholic reunion was just around the corner. The secular news media did a much better job of straight reporting, even interpretation, than the church observers. The lengthy reports in *The New Yorker* were outstanding—even the sophisticates felt called upon to inform their clientele of what the saints were up to.

There were favorable results, too, and these appear to be permanent. At least they have taken hold and are spreading. The cordial treatment of the observers at the council encouraged the Protestant-Catholic dialogue movement which had started before the council was called. The dialogues which I attended or from which I received comprehensive reports were both cordial and on a very high level.

On December 10, 1962, a dialogue was held at the Roman Catholic archdiocesan theological seminary in St. Louis which

I covered for my newspaper. Despite a heavy snowstorm that made driving hazardous, ninety Protestant ministers and seventy-five Catholic priests attended the dinner meeting. Cardinal Joseph E. Ritter, who had returned only that day from the Vatican Council, arrived at the meeting late because the storm slowed up the twenty-mile drive he had to make. He told the clergy that he had made the effort to come in order that he might give the dialogue his blessing. "There will be more dialogues like this," he added. "We Catholics have been slow to do our part in making friends with our non-Catholic brethren."

The most spirited discussion that night was of the variant Catholic and Protestant views of revelation—the Bible and tradition. The Catholic spokesman explained what his church meant by "the unwritten tradition" (Council of Trent, 1546), which is held to be divinely inspired and binding on the Church, as well as the Bible. The spokesman for the Protestant clergy explained why this view of received tradition was unacceptable to Protestants. He also set forth the divergent interpretations of "the infallible Scriptures" among Protestants—modernists and fundamentalists. It was the first time I had ever heard this old thorn of contention brought out when both sides were present. The ministers and priests proved to themselves that they could debate their differences openly, frankly, and in a friendly manner.

These dialogues have been successful because the participants were competent and unfailingly courteous—and because the time was ripe. The old festering questions were asked, and answers and discussion were sharp and clear. There was no dodging. The participants have talked about such subjects as inspiration, holy orders, confessions, and pastoral duties; the questions of the Virgin Mary, the Catholic saints, papal infallibility, marriage, and the education of children. The dialogues have been a most heartening demonstration of the spirit by which a multifaith society can be kept in health. They are an exercise in Christian love at its intellectual best. Many lasting friendships have been formed between participants on both sides.

In the United States, the Catholic Church is growing much faster than the Protestant bodies; it has the very best reasons for believing it will surpass them within a few years. It is also a city church and already dominates the religious scene in most of the larger cities. It is not likely to abandon that position before taking time to see what may become of it and how it will work out. If the shoe were on the other foot, would Protestants do otherwise?

Interfaith relations were improving before the accession of Pope John XXIII, and there is every indication that they will continue to improve. But, for the foreseeable future, they will remain interchurch affairs. It would seem that the first business of those Protestants concerned for church unity is to set their own house in order. Let the new Reformation of a splintering history begin at home. Protestantism may renew its witness too.

The movement for church unity is now in the doldrums. The practical difficulties have proved to be a thousand times more formidable than was foreseen in the recent burst of enthusiasm. Emotional problems—face-saving, pride, nostalgia, and the like —must be dealt with, as well as vested interests in budget, funds, endowment, and bureaucratic tenure. To take a famous example, the Methodist Church has contributed as much talent and more money to interdenominational councils than any other Protestant body. Yet its own family problems of church union are intensely real and exceedingly sensitive, what with its history and its world-wide empire of institution, mission, and responsibility. Are Methodist ministers to be asked to accept reordination as the price of church union? And would the outside world look upon this sacrifice as confession that their orders had alway been fraudulent?

Baptists, the largest body, are organized as free associations of self-governing local congregations—Southern, American, National, Progressive, and other conventions. Presbyterians are federated in a pattern similar to that of the government of our fifty states. The United Church of Christ operates under a new system that combines congregational and presbyterial principles. Eight million Lutherans are divided into ten church groups, and they differ from all the rest in doctrine, liturgy, government, and church practice. The Protestant Episcopal Church is a member of the Anglican communion, whose traditions are deeply embedded in national life and culture in many parts of the world. There are Orthodox churches and clergy in our councils, and they are not Protestants at all. The great and growing body of Pentecostals remains on the outside of councils.

If there are, as reported, two hundred and sixty non-Catholic Christian denominations, we must multiply the problem of unity by that number. Is the job to be done piecemeal, and, if so, where do we start, and how long will it take? During the past ten years I have raised the question with scores of churchmen, clergy and laity, from many denominations in many places. Except for about a year and a half when Pope John and the Vatican Council sent hopes soaring, the best-informed sources were not optimistic for union.

Yet the dream will not die, for reasons that are so overpowering as to appear themselves to be acts of God. The leaders of Christian faith—Catholic, Protestant, and Eastern Orthodox—perceive that their "unholy divisions" are both a scandal in the non-Christian world, at home and abroad, and their greatest source of weakness. What is more, they are heresy. So the conscience is involved; and the churchmen whom I have heard talk about Christian unity made the most of this tender point. The liberal clergy has always held denominational ties lightly, at least as being secondary in importance. Within a single week I saw eight ministers from seven different denominations received into the itinerant ministry of the Methodist Church.

Time was when brethren in Christ, competing for the latest

substantial family to unpack its goods in town, grinned and remarked, "After all, we are all headed for the same place." Today the newcomers are quite likely to take the old admonition at face value and shop around before settling in a new church home; father, mother, and children all get a vote.

Protestant families today are as mobile in religion as with their jobs and house addresses. As a Methodist bishop put it, "Denominationalism has simply lost meaning for the laity." The mushrooming suburban churches which encompass Protestant growth are denominational in name only. Their families show more loyalty to neighborhood than to any religious tradition. Families and individuals move from evangelical "free" churches into the liturgical fold and live and worship happily thereafter. As the old Methodist bishop said, "When a Kansas farmer's income reaches five thousand dollars, he begins to feel longings for the apostolic succession." But moves from high church to low work out quite as well. Mixed marriages are a large factor.

When I first became religion editor of a daily newspaper in 1914, Protestants and Catholics ignored one another's churches except for weddings and funerals; there was no communication in religion. But there was plenty of sniping among the Protestants—across denominational lines, across the middle aisle in divided congregations, and often between pulpit and pew. Proselytizing was a dirty word and a common practice.

Thirty years later, Protestants had called a truce. All the churches that made news, except the Southern Baptists, belonged to local, state, and national councils; the clergy fraternized in their own associations, at community and religious affairs, and on the golf course. I used to receive reams of both Protestant propaganda attacking the Catholic Church and Catholic publications assailing the Protestants. The hostility between the two Christian camps was reflected also in the preaching I heard. It was a dreary business. We have outlived that. There are too many Catholics for Protestants to ignore them. They have lived together too long. Too many of their sons and daughters have attended the same schools, played together, danced to the same music, laughed at the same jokes. Too many of their sons have served together in their country's armed forces, too many are buried all over the world. Come Sunday, they go their separate ways. How separate and why is what we want to know.

# 14

## Sixty-five
## Years in Capsule

From the genteel poverty and ardent pulpiteering of the circuit rider and his unordained colleague in brush arbors to televised masses and Protestant festivals of praise in lordly cathedrals and the Easter parade on Fifth Avenue; from the empire drumbeat of Theodore Roosevelt's bully days to the March on Washington and the march to Rome—this is the sometimes hallowed, sometimes carnival ground we have covered. In two-thirds of a century the world was turned upside down, but not at the hands of Christians—they clung to the status quo and counted their chickens coming home to roost. Religion made news and the day's news made sermons. Nearly everybody got into the act, for religion was not only a system of beliefs and practices but a national pastime. Religion was cowed and diluted by politics, and politics was challenged and kibitzed by religion until the reader of history must get the impression that the two concerns were homogenized beyond separation. In the early years of our period, a frequent visitor at the White House was Roman Catholic Cardinal James Gibbons of Baltimore, calling on his old Protestant friend President Theodore Roosevelt, interceding for the poor, for the organization of labor, and an end to the twelve-hour, seven-day week. In the 1920s it was a Methodist bishop, Francis McConnell, who led the churches' war on the same old evils and spoke up and wrote in behalf of the same forgotten groups in a prosperous nation. In 1965 clergy and lay leaders of the major faiths—Protestant, Catholic, and Jewish—joined hands in Washington to nudge the elbow of President Lyndon B. Johnson in his War on Poverty, with three cheers for the Great Society. Johnson, incidentally, was the first President to be inaugurated with prayers that had been censored for time in order to meet the television schedule. In a multifaith society it was found necessary to insure that eager clergymen did not give to God time that belonged to Caesar.

In our time, the experience of clergy and churches and church councils in politics, and of the politicians with them, has been a mixed blessing, like long prayers and dull sermons. Sometimes one party got his fingers burned, then the other. Early in the century the starry-eyed Social Gospelers saw many of their practical aims for social justice enacted into law, but they were stopped cold by war, by the resistance of entrenched wealth and power, and by the cussedness in poor old human nature. A church lobby won and lost the fight for national prohibition in just thirteen years—1920–1933.

The most disastrous adventure of religion in politics was a reopening of an old Protestant war on Catholics in political life —the sorry record goes back to the early nineteenth century. In 1928, after a scandalous pulpit campaign, the Roman Catholic Alfred E. Smith was buried under an avalanche of prejudice and prohibition zeal. In 1960, with the same religious issue involved but more furtively, another Catholic, John F. Kennedy, won a cliff-hanging race. It now appears that this old issue of a religious qualification for public office has been settled—not many religious controversies have a happy ending.

The historic, bloodstained battle for the Negro American's rights brought church and state together, sometimes in harmony, sometimes in conflict. The national legal victory has yet to be translated into community life. The churches have had more success in winning integration in business and industry,

hotels, restaurants, and theaters than in their own congregations. A happy by-product of this struggle was that it united the
different faiths in a common cause.

The map of the world has changed faster during this century
than in the previous thousand years, and Christian churches
were caught in the upheaval. In 1900 John R. Mott was rallying
the Christian missionary forces for a final campaign "to win the
world for Christ in a single generation." In 1964 Christian missionaries were murdered by native mobs in the Congo. The
Bolshevik revolution of 1917 raised the specter of Communism
in Holy Russia, and the movement has been spreading ever
since—the most powerful foe Christianity has ever faced. In
1949 China was lost to the family of nations and Christian missions that had been at work there for more than a century.

On the home front religion had its usual round of victories,
defeats, and draws. During the first quarter of the century the
old-line denominations remained static; they were torn by dissension over Genesis and the Virgin Birth. But new denominations were springing up by the score—they were churches of the
poor, the Pentecostals filled with the Spirit and looking for the
end of the world, and the do-it-yourself sects.

In California, fountainhead of movements, Babel of religion
and politics, Sister Aimee Semple McPherson emerged from
religious and social obscurity to found the International Church
of the Foursquare Gospel. For nearly twenty years she received
more publicity of a sort than any other preacher or bishop in
the state. She glamourized her Pentecostal creed on a colorful
stage, copied Hollywood stunts, held healing missions, and carried on a professional program of relief for the poor. In 1925
Sister Aimee dedicated the Angelus Temple Church of the
Foursquare Gospel, and her congregations became larger and
more generous. But she became involved in an ocean beach
"kidnaping" scenario of her own account, and the published
versions by the skeptical became so detailed and uninhibited
that the postal authorities had to step in. The mystery of Sister
Aimee's lightweight shoes that showed no mark of her long

desert trek back from captivity has never been solved. She died in 1944 of an overdose of sleeping powders.

The most famous Southern Baptist preacher of the 1920s was J. Frank Norris of the First Baptist Church in Forth Worth, Texas. He was a ripsnorting leader of fundamentalism who found his age "hell-bound" and modernist religion and politics a stand-off for sin. His sensational radio sermons reached a wide audience in the South and Middle West; but he named names, and this brought him enemies and embarrassed his fellow Baptists. Norris was indicted three times during his Fort Worth pastorate but was never convicted. In 1912 he was indicted for arson and perjury after his church had burned. In 1926 he was indicted for murder. Norris admitted shooting a caller in the church pastor's study, a political foe named Chipps. But in court Norris pleaded self-defense and was acquitted. The slaying and the trial received nation-wide publicity.

In the 1930s a familiar voice on a national radio hookup was a Roman Catholic priest who preached a mixture of religion and politics—papal encyclicals and the propaganda of the Farmer-Labor Party. Charles Edward Coughlin was pastor of the Shrine of the Little Flower in Royal Oak, Michigan, and the non-Catholic public had never heard of him until his broadcast remedy for the Depression brought him into the limelight. The American Institute of Public Opinion reported that an average audience of three and a half million men and women listened to Father Coughlin's Sunday-afternoon broadcast. His voice ranged from dulcet tenderness, as he extolled the old-fashioned Christian virtues, to raucous belligerency in demands for reforms in capitalism and representative government. But his social-political platform was confined to vague generalities —his own summary was *Social Justice*. He published a magazine with that name. He demanded that the government "restore silver to its proper value," but never said what its proper value was.

Father Coughlin was at first a vociferous supporter of President Franklin D. Roosevelt and the New Deal—"It is Roosevelt or ruin!" He denounced the "international bankers," and praised the President for "driving the money-changers from the temple." But in 1936 he turned against the administration, calling the President "Franklin Double-Cross Roosevelt." In that year's national campaign, Father Coughlin supported a third-party candidate for President, United States Representative William Lemke, who polled 891,000 votes.

In the later years of his radio and publishing career, Father Coughlin charged that Jews created the Soviet Union and were behind the international Communist movement. He was denounced by many prominent Catholics, including the former governor of New York, Alfred E. Smith. In April 1942 his magazine *Social Justice* was barred from the mails by Postmaster General Frank C. Walker for violating the Espionage Act of 1917 in attacking the national war effort. The magazine ceased publication. Father Coughlin's ecclesiastical superiors halted his public career, and he retired to parish duties.

The Ku Klux Klan was revived in the period between the two world wars—in the late 1920s it claimed a membership of five million. Its secret oath and sheets and hoods were reserved for native-born white Protestants, and it drew wide support from church congregations and clergy, North and South.

The Depression of the 1930s drew more churches, church councils, and clergy into the public arena than any other national emergency except war. Ministers presided over community soup kitchens, and their church women collected clothing and household goods for needy families. Ministers also took the lead in many states and local communities in campaigns for public aid to the distressed. John Steinbeck's *The Grapes of Wrath* became the most widely quoted novel in sermons since Charles M. Sheldon's *In His Steps*, published in 1896—the earthy talk of Steinbeck's Dust Bowl characters was passed over.

Next to the involvement of churches and clergy in the Negro revolution, perhaps the profoundest spiritual experience of the American Protestant clergy is the movement in our time into the ranks of pacifism. This is a break with the past, the past in which chaplains of the armed forces were expected to preach the doctrine of immortality so young men in uniform would be unafraid to die. Religious pacifism is older than Christianity, but until the end of World War I the movement had extremely slow growth in the United States. Quakers have always exerted an influence out of all proportion to their small number. But the religious climate was unfavorable and generally hostile to pacifism in the clergy; patriotism was too strong, and the established churches enjoyed the patronage of the political power structure. In World War I the churches enlisted in the nation's all-out effort. Nearly all the clergy went along, and there were not many conscientious objectors. But by 1941 there were a great number of pacifist ministers, and many more conscientious objectors appeared among the draftees for combat duty. In 1957 a lifetime pacifist clergyman, Edwin T. Dahlberg, was elected president of the National Council of Churches.

In October 1944, in a hotel coffee shop in Williston, North Dakota, I met a group of conscientious objectors from a camp nearby. The young men were employed for the duration of the war on an irrigation project. It was Sunday and they had been to Sunday school and church. We talked for two hours—I had two sons and three sons-in-law in the armed forces. The CO's were a happy crew, browned and physically fit from their outdoor labor. Two of them were preministerial students, two had been teaching school; the others, as I remember, were university and professional-school students. All had Protestant faith in common.

What impressed me most was not the high morale of the conscientious objectors, but the friendliness of the townspeople and farmers toward them; the young men told me there had never been an unpleasant incident. Of course many Williston men had gone off to war.

The next week I visited a German prisoner-of-war work camp on a sugar beet ranch in Nebraska. Fifty prisoners were topping the beets which had been plowed up, using wicked-looking, short-handled, curved knives with which a strong man could have beheaded a horse. The only guard was a tall, slender, young American soldier with a rifle; he was leaning against a fence, half-asleep. Each prisoner was stripped to the waist, his skin bronzed by the sun. They were powerful fellows, built like American football players. They laughed, joked, and sang as they swung their knives. The farmer who took me to see his beet harvest told me that the prisoners' wages were being held for them till after the war. He also said he had to forbid the Germans from going into his cornfields while naked to the waist, as the sharp blades of corn would slash their skin and draw blood. The prisoners argued with him, and thought it would be fun.

CO's and POW's survived their countries' war on hard work, the best food, and laughter.

I interviewed for my newspaper the late United States Senator George W. Norris at his modest home in McCook, Nebraska, where Standard time changes from Central to Mountain, as shown on two big clocks in the Burlington station. Norris was alone, and we sat in the big living room, which was warmed by a low fire in the fireplace; my host served candy and apples and, before I left, coffee. On the low coffee table were a thumbed Bible, a volume of Shakespeare, and copies of *The Christian Century*, *The Churchman* (Norris was an Episcopalian), *Harper's*, and *Atlantic Monthly*. A neighbor brought a load of firewood, and Norris went out in the yard to show him where to stack it.

Norris reminisced on his long career in Congress—in the House of Representatives from 1903 to 1913 and in the Senate from 1913 to 1942, when he was defeated for the first time. He told the long story of his successful fight in the House to liberalize the rules and take dictatorial powers from Speaker Joseph G. Cannon. Another liberal like himself in the Senate was the late Albert J. Beveridge of Indiana. Norris admired his talent and courage, but said, "Beveridge was the most conceited man I ever knew; he never overlooked an opportunity to humiliate a fellow senator and praise his own speeches." The pride of Norris's public life was the leading role he took in establishing the Tennessee Valley Authority.

George Norris was an old man, eighty-three; his health was failing—he had less than a year to live. And he was the unhappiest man I ever saw. The deep gloom in his eyes and on his face as he stirred the ashes of his notable memory was painful to watch. His defeat in 1942 had broken his heart. Yet there was not one word of bitterness in his speech.

Senator Norris's career is dramatic proof of how war that is supposed to unite a nation actually splits public opinion, sets one man's mind and conviction against another's, provokes an anguished crisis for Christian faith, and even divides a man's heart, setting one part of him against the other. Norris was seeking reconciliation and peace before nightfall.

Norris had opposed United States entry into World War I, an act of courage that brought him bitter and inflammatory denunciation, rebuffs in public and private. He came up for re-election in 1918, and the war party and the superpatriots whetted their long knives for his scalp. Norris went home to Nebraska, hired a hall in Omaha, and acted as his own chairman and introduced himself. For more than two hours he stood on the big, bare stage and talked to his old neighbors and friends and constituents. He was no orator, but no candidate for public office ever received closer attention as he defended his vote against the war resolution. His fellow citizens heard him out, then went home and voted for him. Norris returned to the Senate for twenty-four more years of distinguished service.

In 1942 the country was again at war with Germany, and Norris supported the war administration and its war measures. In 1944 I talked to dozens of Norris's old constituents and supporters in Omaha and Lincoln, in county-seat towns, in villages and on farms. I also spoke with a few men who had worked for him in earlier campaigns. Most of them had the same story: Norris was defeated in 1942 because the people of Nebraska felt that he had deserted them and turned against himself. They believed he had been right in 1918 and wrong in 1941.

This part of my interview with George Norris was deleted by my managing editor at the old *St. Louis Star-Times*.

The Protestant pacifist clergy followed the example of George Norris in reverse—most of the older ministers supported First World War, then attended to their religious duties in the Second. And the heavens of public wrath didn't fall on many heads.

The Korean War was a shocking, humbling, humiliating experience, a bitter cup. There was no victory, only a stalemate; and under the emotional strain of this crisis—new in the nation's history—the people turned to religion and their churches and against their political leaders.

A spectacular boom in religion was under way before the end of the Korean War; it began to level off in about ten years. Church attendance, membership, contributions, and new church construction rose to record highs, and religious discussions became increasingly popular on college campuses.

Profound changes appeared in church life. Preaching became more critical of national aims and practices, and for the first time the clergy was more skeptical of political behavior than the laity. There was renewed study of the Bible and theology; for the first time since colonial days, laymen were studying theology and church history with the help of their ministers, professors from theological seminaries, and professionally prepared publications of their denominations.

The spectacle of deacons and elders and trustees in classes of religion was something new. So was the theology they studied. It was no longer Hip, Hip, Hurrah! for our side. The green pastures of the hallelujah faith had been invaded by the gloomy prophets of the postwar Continental theology that rates man low as a sinner, ambivalent by nature, and punctures his balloon of pride. Karl Barth and Reinhold Niebuhr had taken all the fun out of writing ringing resolutions for progress and peace. Fifty years ago Sigmund Freud made it bad judgment to tell about our dreams—it had always been bad taste. The new theology makes personal professions of sanctity embarrassing.

Church architecture led music and the other arts on the march into the twentieth century: modern functional style in place of Gothic cavernous gloom and aspiration; Bach over Fanny Crosby; impressionism in stained glass and stainless steel; pulpits demoted; churches in the round.

Religious education became a full-time profession for men and women with graduate degrees instead of a one-hour Sunday-morning stint for pious old maids. Religious drama became the vogue, taking the stage from cardboard-and-shirttail pageants. Real animals appeared in the Christmas crèche on the church lawn.

Other revolutions in the religious field confused the historic relations of church and state, making everybody feel at home. The Roman Catholic Church emerged in the mainstream of American life. Protestant domination of public affairs ended before word of it got around. The nation's piety was stamped on its coins. To some religionists, the Supreme Court was thrust upon the throne of Antichrist. Prayers at football games, public auctions, and state fairs survived in the South.

Preaching in the past sixty-five years has been a running commentary on the fast-moving events of a hectic time for a generous people who were dragged into the worldstream against their will and have had rough going ever since—from the spit-and-polish Spanish-American War to the dirty, frustrating guerrilla hide-and-seek in South Vietnam. Our period opened with patrician sermons on foreign missions and Christian responsibility (*noblesse oblige*) for the whole world—"the white man's burden." In 1965 the emphasis is a reverse reading of the old hallelujah faith—the white man's burden is his colored neighbor. The pulpit has found a theme on which Protestant, Catholic, and Jew can unite. Instead of missionary barrels, funds are raised to bail out sit-in demonstrators, marchers, and volunteer civil rights workers. Church and state share the burden of conscience and reform, and the villains of the piece are status-minded property owners and realtors.

Protestant preaching ran on three parallel tracks that can be distinguished even in the fire and smoke of controversy: evangelistic; sermons on current topics; and low-pitched little homilies to go with liturgical worship. The three lines crisscrossed, of course, especially in times of crisis, of which there have been a God's plenty. In my visits to many churches, I found the differences were less in 1964 than in 1910. The rise of the middle class, popular education, and the mass media took care of that.

The evangelical track was straight and narrow; the business of preaching was to convert sinners, baptize them, and enroll them as church members. What could be less controversial? But it did not work out that way. The evangelicals and fundamentalists have had no more success at staying out of feuds than the rest. Their otherworldly faith has always embroiled them in debate—pulpit, platform, and press—over doctrine, biblical interpretation, and church government. Their rural-oriented moral code has kept them in a running—and losing—battle with changing social customs. The success of revivalism has been grossly exaggerated. I have visited cities and towns and rural communities where the revival churches had counted more converts than there were people.

The record of preaching Christian ethics is long, wide, and honorable. Walter Rauschenbusch was the most famous pioneer of the Social Gospel at the beginning of the period. His humanitarian aims are now taken for granted, and each one is resisted wherever it clashes with local custom, prejudice, and vested interest. This prophetic school of preaching is like a world's fair where fresh visitors are always coming in and weary patrons going out; and, after two thousand years, the world doesn't look saved. It is popular in the sense that it is not recondite; it speaks to the people, applying the teachings of the Old Testament prophets and of Jesus to contemporary problems. But it was never popular in the sense that it carried congregations with it. This lag between pulpit and pew means that liberal preaching is forever in crisis.

The fifteen-minute homilies buried in high-church liturgy have been heard by more Christian communicants than all the sermons of revivalists and Social Gospelers put together, as the church yearbooks plainly show. The patrician discourses from 1880 to 1930 were intended to confirm the elect in their feeling of superiority. That beautiful arrangement has been rudely upset, like white supremacy. The Catholic priest has now been instructed to pep up his sermons but keep them short. The Protestant minister whose patrician congregation has fled to the suburbs—the last stand of segregation and style—faces a terrifying task. The national religious wanderlust has trampled down the old signboards of denominationalism. The pastor must be as agile as an old hen trying to mother a brood of ducks. He is well-treated as "one of us," but he had better know his way around in a house of many mansions. He must write one sermon and deliver it without irritant for the steel and iron executive who was a Presbyterian segregationist, the disappointed clerk from Rochester who went to school with Negroes and the sons of immigrants, the retired farmer and his wife from Nebraska who dislike all foreigners and foreign missions, and the graduate student from U.C.L.A. who believes that all religious differences are a matter of semantics. All the ingredients for a first-class Donnybrook must jell at the coffee hour.

In the early 1900s preaching was the first business of the church. It was not all top quality, but its claim on first place was undisputed. Men were called to preach. The ministry becomes more and more specialized, like medicine and advertising copy, and few general practitioners are left who find their chief satisfaction in the pulpit. (This is the biggest change I have seen in the practice of the old profession.) More young men and women are going to theological seminaries, but the seminaries are turning out fewer preachers. And members of the younger generation of pastors with churches do not really enjoy preaching; they kiss it off as a quaint chore. They do not enjoy church conventions, except the socializing. They are bored by routine pastoral calling. And they loathe church business. They are expert in liturgy—their scripture readings are long and their prayers short.

The terrifying thing about their career in the ministry, the burden of the proud and sensitive spirit that breaks so many gifted men, is the bleak uncertainty that overhangs everything mortal. They find inspiration and refreshment in the small company of the elect—like-minded ministers and other eggheads. But their congregations, liberal or conservative in theology, have this in common—their resistance to change is glacial; they appear to their minister as taking special delight in persisting in the sins of their fathers; the immemorial conflict and estrangement between clergy and laity is handed down like the family Bible. The current movement for "more participation by the laity in church life" really means that ordained ministers are expendable. They may serve but they cannot lead.

How do churches and congregations "get that way"? Granitic, immovable, set in their ways. How does it happen, as I have seen so many times, that a power bloc agglutinates within a congregation, comes to dominate the church's life, hold all the offices, merely passing them around and weaving a hair shirt for any minister who may arrive with new ideas, sympathies, and broader concerns?

In my youth there was a doggerel couplet about frozen churches:

"Our church has stood a hundred years or so,
And to every new suggestion we always answered NO!"

Or there is the take-off on the Tory in secular affairs:

"Nothing must ever be tried for the first time."

I'm old enough to remember when people stood on the sidewalk and jeered at the driver of a stalled automobile: "You'd better get a horse." As the horse-and-buggy public eyed them nothing could have been more laughable than those "queer-looking gas buggies."

Recently I visited an old church, with beautiful property, which I have known for three generations of its membership. I counted forty-four persons at Sunday worship where many times I used to see more than two hundred. The church has had a succession of seven pastors in the past twenty-five years. The membership and Sunday school and youth groups and women's association are fading fast. The same half-dozen families are running the church who ran it thirty years ago. Members of these ramrod families are social pals, and they club together to dominate their church. The minister doesn't have a chance; he knows in advance what the vote will be on any proposal he might make.

An informed layman gives his explanation of the stand-pattism in local churches: "Despite the rise in church membership after World War II, the hard core of lay leadership didn't change too much—didn't expand enough to make room for the new members, who had to accept the old entrenched cliques." (Church and synagogue membership in the country rose to 121,000,000 by the end of 1963, the last year for which the statistics are available. The total is an increase of more than 3,000,000 over 1962.)

The interested and worried layman goes on to say: "A certain type of personality tends to become a 'pillar of the church'—usually mature men and women with few competing outside interests. But these graying work horses are a dwindling group —the old Protestant power elite which, during the first third of the century, was the social Establishment at national and local levels has been yielding stubbornly—and grumpily—to the great urban, secular, trifaith body in our multifaith population. The younger clergy realize that the future of Protestantism does not lie with the aging apologists and pillars of a church past—a period that has passed forever. The clergy are also more sensitive than their retirement-age lay leaders to the erosion of an effective Protestant witness in competition with a modernized, aggressive Catholic Church, or with galloping secularism."

A retired denominational executive who presided over some two hundred churches for twenty years told me that during his term many of those churches sent the same delegates to every convention year after year. In most cases they were either retired men of means, and their wives, or high-placed business executives who made their own work schedules. The denominational officer said that the presence of "so many mossbacks" meant that every convention was weighted heavily on the side of ultraconservatism.

There is of course a deeper, harder to get at reason for the religious "resistance to change." Religious faith is by its very nature a clinging to the past, an ancient past. It is devotion to what was handed down by the fathers: the Scriptures, traditions, forms of worship, clerical orders, and a manual of arms for national and local church organization. During the past sixty-five years, the terrible stresses of the times—wars and troubled truces, international and racial conflicts—have placed these ancient spiritual and moral values and mores on the defensive; the past was made to appear rosier than it was. The present-day venerable fathers among churchmen have now been living for two generations in anxiety, and this has added emotional drive to their fear of change.

Rabbi Solomon B. Freehof, in a sermon at the installation of another rabbi, said, "The function of the minister in the congregation is to build up the love of life, to deepen the consolations of human companionships, and to strengthen the charm of human hope." There are no Gallup polls, no Hooper ratings, to tell the minister at the end of a church year how things went with his preaching, what the box score was. He may add and subtract membership rolls and run the totals on attendance and offerings. But concerning the effectiveness of his preaching, who can tell?

Pope John XXIII, not long before his death, gave some advice on preaching. He told the parish priests of Rome that their sermons should not be "a sequence of empty formulas" but should cover faith, morals, culture, and creed. He was quoted in press dispatches as saying, "It is certain that the word of God touches men of every age and condition with the intimate goodness it brings with it. There is, however, also the art of interesting and uplifting the congregation. This is an art which must adapt itself to the historic and cultural requirements of every age."

I heard or read that statement of the ideal in preaching from at least a dozen Protestant ministers. But I didn't hear much of it put to practice. Preaching is no longer an art, except with a few masters who appear old-fashioned; it isn't interesting; whether such copybook preaching is "uplifting to the congregation," I wouldn't know.

What is the picture of church life that the religious newswriters see in 1965? The scene is fresh, exciting, and in some areas revolutionary. There is vigor and invention and the confusion that always accompanies a break with the past. Two factors stand out:

First, the cast of characters is new. Church life is now dominated by professionals, men and women who have taken long years of academic and specialized studies. They have already developed their peculiar parlance, which sometimes reads like the Latin on a doctor's prescription. They also enjoy a camaraderie that is new and wonderfully productive in ideas and methods. New names and faces appear with greater frequency —the retirement rule serves youth.

Second, the clergy and the denominational leaders by and large are taking the church to the people. They are not satisfied to ring the bell and wait for the congregation to appear. This spirit of initiative—taking the offensive—is revolutionary. It has the vigorous backing of church councils from the national to the local level. It covers home and foreign missions as well as parish activities.

There are today more than seventeen million Americans

sixty-five years of age or older, and the churches have taken their special needs as a major religious responsibility. I have visited several churches where the new provision for elderly persons was a year-round activity, and it served the community, not just the church membership. Denominations and local churches underwrite modern housing for the old-age group and provide for the physical, intellectual, and spiritual needs of the residents.

Longevity and automation have made leisure time a staggering problem and exposed the unpreparedness of public and private agencies to deal with it. Churches and clergy are taking a leading hand in the drive to banish loneliness and neglect and make the last years, the idle years, congenial, happy, and fruitful.

Churches on the home front have at last faced up to the problems of health, as their foreign missionaries did from the beginning. This new church concern includes not only physical culture and professional counseling in mental health, child guidance, and family life, but psychiatry and allied services. I have attended church counseling sessions at which ministers, psychiatrists, and social workers shared the program. We have come a long way from the days when the circuit rider comforted a troubled farmer in his cornfield or the big-city pastor tried to befriend a juvenile prisoner in the workhouse.

One of the church's tasks is to provide the motivation that school dropouts desperately need. Where the inner life of the person is a factor—the will or the lack of it, self-respect, dignity—there religion and faith may become the organizing principle, the spark of new life. Clergy and lay persons are being trained in this new field. I have visited churches and church-sponsored community centers where the problem of dropouts engaged much of the time and patience and skill of staff members seven days a week.

The churches have re-entered the field of higher education where they had suffered severe setbacks and agonizing frustration. Organized religion had been virtually expelled from many institutions of higher education which the denominations founded and nurtured. For the undergraduates, faith was confined to the study of comparative religion. The denominations have regained some of that lost ground. Attractive church centers for worship and study and the students' social life have won a respected place on the campuses, and they are competently staffed. The united campus ministry, in which several denominations pool their resources, is fully established, and its rightful place and honor are secure. These new church centers on the campuses are also performing a signal service in bringing together the different races, nationalities, and creeds that have become a familiar part of the campus scene.

The historic empire of Christian missions is in revolution too, and in a tragic replay of the earliest church history, the blood of modern martyrs is seeding the soil. What used to be called home and foreign missions are becoming one great mission of service at home and abroad. New national Christian churches have sprung up, and they are running their own show. The new posture of the missionary enterprise is not that of a conqueror but of a friend. Instead of gunboats backing up its piety, it now relies on carpenters' tools, plows, medical skills, instruments, and medications; teaching, preaching (where it is permitted), under the nationals whom the revolution has thrown to the top.

The new drive of Christian churches is bearing down hard on the great areas of modern life—the inner city, the suburb, and exurbia. Suburban living is not new, but its fantastic development in the past fifty years attracted the churches like a magnet, with new buildings and personnel. So promising was the field that the denominations fell over themselves in their hurry to stake out claims. In the old cities and towns and rural areas the churches must recover lost ground.

Edwin T. Dahlberg has had a notable career as a pastor of urban congregations. "We have a special responsibility to step up the pastoral ministry," he says. "Churches today are bigger than they were a generation ago. Communities around the church are more crowded. This quality of size and bigness subjects us to the danger of becoming impersonal. Before we know it, people are lost and lonely. People everywhere are starved for love. Forgotten and passed by, they become resentful and brooding. It is our responsibility as Christians to bring the love of God into the hearts of these lonely people."

Protestants and Catholics and Jews today are trying to bring pastoral care to millions of city people who have no mark of religion that shows. They are really lost.

Is the church doing its part in the great social struggles that face us? Paul Ylvisaker, director of the public affairs program of the Ford Foundation, told an urban session of the General Convention of the Protestant Episcopal Church, held in St. Louis in October 1964: "Now, by default, it is the state which has declared war on poverty, not the church. It is the state . . . which has declared war on crime, not the church. The state has declared war on injustice and intolerance and discrimination and extremism. The church is joining the ranks, but with more draftees than volunteers." According to Ylvisaker, today's basic human needs are for dignity and motivation.

Churches and church councils and home missions are not entirely inactive in trying to meet those needs. In St. Louis, a staff of four ministers from different denominations serves a low-income, high-rise housing project from 8 A.M. to midnight six days a week. In another city the council of churches sponsors a ministry to lonely persons of the upper-income bracket in a luxury apartment house. Another council of churches carries on a chaplaincy service to hospitals, nursing homes, homes for the aged, and penal institutions—and trains the staff by the highest professional standards. An interdenominational group of churches holds special after-school classes for children who are in trouble in school and likely candidates for the dropout group.

Other action programs include chaplains at juvenile courts, vacations in the country for tenement children, health clinics, professional counseling for squabbling families, literacy classes and English classes for the foreign-born, Bible classes, prayer groups, and regular healing missions. This list does not, of course, cover the historic institutions of mercy and healing and help of all major faiths. What the list does show is that the churches now have a new thrust in their traditional mission—they are taking it to the people.

Suburban churches of high-income and status-minded congregations have taken a lot of kicking around, some of it in this book. They represent a real problem, but also a challenge. Here is the testimony of a pastor and denominational officer who has served a very large church in an exclusive community for eleven years with outstanding success and a minimum of friction. "When I came here, the worst threat to the church's integrity of Christian witness and to my own peace of mind was a pagan exaltation of family life. Parents were consumed by the passion for family welfare and happiness, and they looked to their church and minister to solve all their problems. The men were generous and the women were tireless workers. But they were all property-minded. They just couldn't buy enough beautiful and expensive things for their church. The people overwhelmed me and my family with generosities, too. But I don't think they ever gave a thought to what I was supposed to preach or what I was doing there. I went with the property."

I was in position to watch the progress of that minister and his up-and-coming congregation. He gave sermons and week-night talks on medical missions, and the doctors, dentists, nurses, and social workers in his church bought hospital equipment and drugs and shipped them to missions in Asia and Africa. He had equal success with the women; they gave regular support to home and foreign missions for family welfare, child welfare, the care of mothers and infants, health, sanitation, preparation of food, education, child guidance clinics, birth control, and psychiatric treatment. And the men and women became acquainted with the field personnel of half a dozen different denominational and interchurch missions. They had been in the habit of thinking of missions as an institution like Santa Claus or the Community Chest.

I heard quotes and discussions of that man's sermons at district meetings of women of his denomination and at churchmen's meetings. His church multiplied its gifts to missions five times and maintained that record. The congregation doubled its annual contribution to the National Council of Churches in spite of the fact that most of the men disagreed with the Council's pronouncements on public affairs. The minister was asked by the elders to preach a series of sermons on the promise of church union. Most of the people take Protestant unity for granted—they came to that church from twenty-two different denominations, and no church at all, and could not care less about denominational ties.

The minister persuaded his congregation to raise ten thousand dollars for an inner-city project for Negroes and to send ten college students to a summer work camp of the World Council of Churches in Mexico.

The congregation is still captive to the country club atmosphere of the community and hides the same old batch of race prejudices. But it has a guilty conscience. Its refined version of the nineteenth-century Christianity of *noblesse oblige* is meeting human needs.

In town and country life the new thrust of the churches in action is channeled in two directions. The precipitous drop in the rural population and the pockets of poverty that contain many of the survivors have compelled jealous denominations to pool their limited resources in common programs. Five white steeples pointing the way to heaven for five hundred separated Christians is not only a scandal to the faith but an intolerable drain on the purse. And second, town and country parishes with a denominational stamp are a larger, community-wide enterprise, and this brings adequate buildings and a stable, competent ministry. The new day in town and country church life thrives in Vermont, South Dakota, and Nevada; in Texas,

Florida, and California; in prosperous farming areas of the Middle West; and in Appalachia. It has become a national movement.

I have visited Catholic priests serving parishes of poverty-stricken families in abandoned mining communities in the Ozarks. Today their little parishes, some of them a hundred years old, are a home-missions obligation of the archdiocese, drawing regular support from city churches.

I have visited young Lutheran pastors just out of seminary who were organizing new parishes in the Rocky Mountain region or in new communities created by government defense installations. These present-day pioneer preachers start their gospel career with no meetingplace, no house, and no congregation.

On a cold, rainy Sunday the old frame church in a small river town was filled for the nine o'clock service. It was held at that early hour because the minister had a second service at eleven in another church ten miles away. The congregation in the wallpapered sanctuary was largely made up of families, not couples and individuals, and most of them would stay for Sunday school at ten o'clock. There were four generations of town and farm families. The marriage relationships within that congregation were an undecipherable maze; no pastor of record ever fully mastered it.

The name of the little old man in the pulpit had never appeared on a church news page except in his home-town weekly. This was his last pastorate before retirement, but he was preaching only new sermons. He was one of the multitude of clergy who never win acclaim. The main-line denominations would lose half their congregations, in fact they would not have survived, without the quiet, unadvertised, miserably paid services of these gentle souls whose names are written only in the Book of Life. This hardy breed has built churches and blessed people from shore to shore; these men swapped horses and saddlebags for secondhand cars and trailers and kept moving; they have carried the heaviest burden of spreading the Good

News from the day of Pentecost. They recruited candidates for the ministry from congregations where a high-school diploma was a rarity; and the steady decline of the little churches they served brought about a proportionate decline in the number of promising young men entering theological seminaries. Suburban church families have more practical plans for their pampered sons.

The excellent sermon I heard that day was on the subject of God's help in sorrow. It was read freely from manuscript and took twenty minutes. Except for its shorter length, it reminded me of the first sermons I ever heard in the one-room frame church that was built within reach of a small fort to secure the families and livestock against Indian raids and alarms. And it was a much better sermon than I have generally heard in million-dollar temples. The order of worship had not been tinkered with in a century; it consisted of a long Bible lesson, a prayer, hymns for the congregation, an anthem by the volunteer choir, and the collection.

Through all the years, the church as a house of worship and religious instruction and as a center of community life has remained at the heart of American life: in a clearing in the woods with the burial ground outside the plain windows; on street corners in little towns where the only Sunday-morning traffic was to and from church; in brick and stone buildings on city boulevards where the rumble of subway trains disturbed the pastoral prayer. The church still belongs to the quiet in the land who pay their taxes and tend their gardens and their children. The building is handsomer and more comfortable; the music is better and the sermon shorter; and there is less show of emotion than when I was a boy—people weep, but not on Sunday morning in church. Here children learn the story of their parents' faith, and the story is much better told than it was sixty-five years ago. Here the Lord's Supper is celebrated by the Book, young couples are married and receive their friends in the church parlor, infants and converts are baptized, and the dead are honored. Such folkways are not easily broken.

## About the Author

John T. Stewart is an ordained Methodist minister who has served as a pastor of Methodist and Congregational churches for twenty-three years. Born on a fifty-acre farm in Thompsonville, Illinois, the son of a minister and the youngest of twelve children, Mr. Stewart attended McKendree College and the Harvard Divinity School. He is a veteran newspaperman, and for many years was Religion Editor of the St. Louis *Post-Dispatch*. He has also been a teacher of American history and English in high school and junior college, and during World War II was area director of the Farm Security Administration, first in Southeast Missouri and later in Cincinnati.

Mr. Stewart is married and the father of five children. Since his retirement in 1963, he has been acting news editor of the *United Church Herald* and has served as interim pastor of the Grace Presbyterian Church, Crystal City, Missouri.